MARY PROVINCIATTO & PAULO CAROLI

SPRINT by SPRINT

MARY PROVINCIATTO & PAULO CAROLI

SPRINT by SPRINT

Transforming a group of people into a high-performing product team

caroli.org

Translation and revision
Mary Provinciatto and Paulo Caroli

Editorial coordination
Algo Novo Editorial

Graphic design, layout, and cover
Vanessa Lima

Copyright © 2023 by
Mary Provinciatto and Paulo Caroli
All rights in this edition are
reserved to Editora Caroli.
Corcovado, 210 – Jardim Botânico,
Rio de Janeiro, RJ, 22460-050, Brazil
www.caroli.org/editora 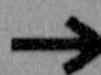
contato@caroli.org

International Catalog Data in Publication (CIP)
(Câmara Brasileira do Livro, SP, Brasil)

Provinciatto, Mary
    Sprint by Sprint: Transforming a group of people into a high-performing product team / Mary Provinciatto, Paulo Caroli. — 1ª ed. — Rio de Janeiro : Editora Caroli, 2023.

ISBN 978-65-86660-26-5

1. Business 2. Agile Software Development 3. Work groups - Business 4. Lean (Product development) 5. Products - Development 6. Products - Project 7. Projects - Methodology 8. Scrum (Product development) 9. Team work I. Caroli, Paulo. II. Title.

23-144993   CDD 658.4022

Index to systematic catalog:
1. Work teams : Business   658.4022

Henrique Ribeiro Soares - Librarian - CRB-8/9314

ACKNOWLEDGMENTS

We thank the agile community for participating in this book. Your comments and feedback were essential to improving the content. We thank everyone who participated in the polls that helped us choose the title and the book cover. Thanks to the people on the many teams we worked with. Our interactions and learning together gave us the motivation to write and to share the knowledge described here.

Thanks also to ThoughtWorks for their leadership and positive examples, practices, and attitudes. Many people know ThoughtWorks as a leading global technology company and a fine example of using agility and best practices to develop digital products, but for us, their greatest impact has been in their commitment to respecting and developing people's skills, competencies, and minds.

We also wish to thank our family and friends, the dear people who support us in our daily work. Your support was critical in the creation and evolution of this book.

INDEX

FOREWORD →

like to play sports — baseball, tennis, pickleball, basketball, and my current favorite, bicycling. I grew up with two younger brothers in a neighborhood of mostly boys who liked to gather in a churchyard near-by and play whatever depending on who brought what equipment that day. However, I've never really enjoyed watching sports. I do find, though, that if I'm at someone's house for a Super Bowl party that if the sports casters are especially knowledgeable and/or entertaining that I can be drawn in to follow the action. The sports casters are key. It's not the game itself but having someone explain and call attention to the highlights. In *Sprint by Sprint*, Mary and Paulo are just like superb sportscasters. They are experienced players themselves so they, like the TV talking heads, are seasoned veterans of the sport they are describing, Mary and Paulo point out the important facets of the game as it is being played and do an excellent job of wrapping up at the end.

The game here, of course, is software development and the play-by-play in their new book is the report of six months of work by a distributed team. Mary and Paul keep the reader entertained, informed and learning from "watching" the progress of others. You will see the slip-ups and the celebrations. You can "boo" or "cheer" as you like. This is honest, transparent broadcasting in real life with no cover-ups or minimizing of strategic errors. This is the best way to learn — in my humble opinion.

This book works for newbies because the introductory material is good but can easily be skipped, like refusing an appetizer off the menu. For those who need extra helpings, it's possible to dive in and spend extra time learning the history and the ins and outs of any play on the field.

At any point in the game, as I often do if I'm watching a sport I don't understand, you can turn to the authors for help. When something particularly arcane has me puzzled, I will ask a trusted companion at a game, "Why did that happen?" or "What was the team trying to accomplish with that move?" This is not Monday Morning Quarterbacking where 50-50 hindsight makes the commentator seem so much wiser than the professional coach or players. This is good, solid, helpful information based on the practices and experiences of the authors. Mary and Paulo have made this book seem like an old friend, ready to open and read about any troubling issue.

The book works for distributed teams as well as those who are co-located. Distributed teams were with us before the pandemic and will be with us as long as there are development teams of any kind. We have all learned to be agile in facing this challenge, but we can all be better. There are some wonderful tips and techniques demonstrated by the team in *Sprint by Sprint* for dealing with distributed issues.

The book ends by applying the best possible closing for any project — reflection. Since Norm Kerth built the practice of retrospectives on the work of Virginia Satir, a family therapist, those of us who work in software development have used this ritual to learn and grow. Mary and Paulo ask the hard questions about their own work, trying to learn as much as possible to help with the next adventure. What worked well that we don't want to forget? What should we do differently? What still puzzles us? What did we learn?

I believe you're going to enjoy the play-by-play of this team's story. You'll laugh. You'll cry. You'll groan. You'll cheer. You'll have a great time and learn a lot. You can't ask for more than that! Enjoy!

Linda Rising, *speaker, author, consultant*
lindarising.org.

WHAT YOU NEED TO KNOW BEFORE READING THIS BOOK

The book covers six months of work performed by a team developing a digital product, specifically a Software Development Kit (SDK) for Android and iOS. Our goal with this book is to share the challenges and lessons learned since the first week, the first delivery into production until the end of the consulting engagement.

The team consisted of people from different companies and locations: some came from the consulting company ThoughtWorks, based in Porto Alegre, Brazil, and some were from the client's organization, located in another city. The team composition was as follows:

>> An Agile consultant for the first six weeks of the engagement (Paulo Caroli).

>> An Engagement Manager/ Scrum Master (Mary Provinciatto).

>> Seven software developers.

>> A UX Designer.

>> A Product Owner.

This book is divided into five main sections:

>> *Technical and theoretical content:* offers additional material that will help you get more out of the book. If you are unfamiliar with the agile world of digital products, we recommend that you read this section first. However, even if you are already part of this world, you can use this entire section to clarify any doubts, and learn a little more.

>> *The day-to-day of a product team in action:* Was written based on actual team communication and is organized chronologically. The information presented on the day the communication took place will be the title of the chapter, so you can follow the team's daily routine and observe when and how each concept and each conversation emerged. This section is divided into parts that represent each week of the engagement.

>> *Issues and recommendations:* After the six weeks of engagement, we present a short list of the biggest issues and recommendations related to how the team was working.

>> *The next four months:* Summarizes the main events that occurred in the last months of the engagement.

>> *Additional knowledge:* Here we offer some resources and templates to make your reading and learning experience even more complete.

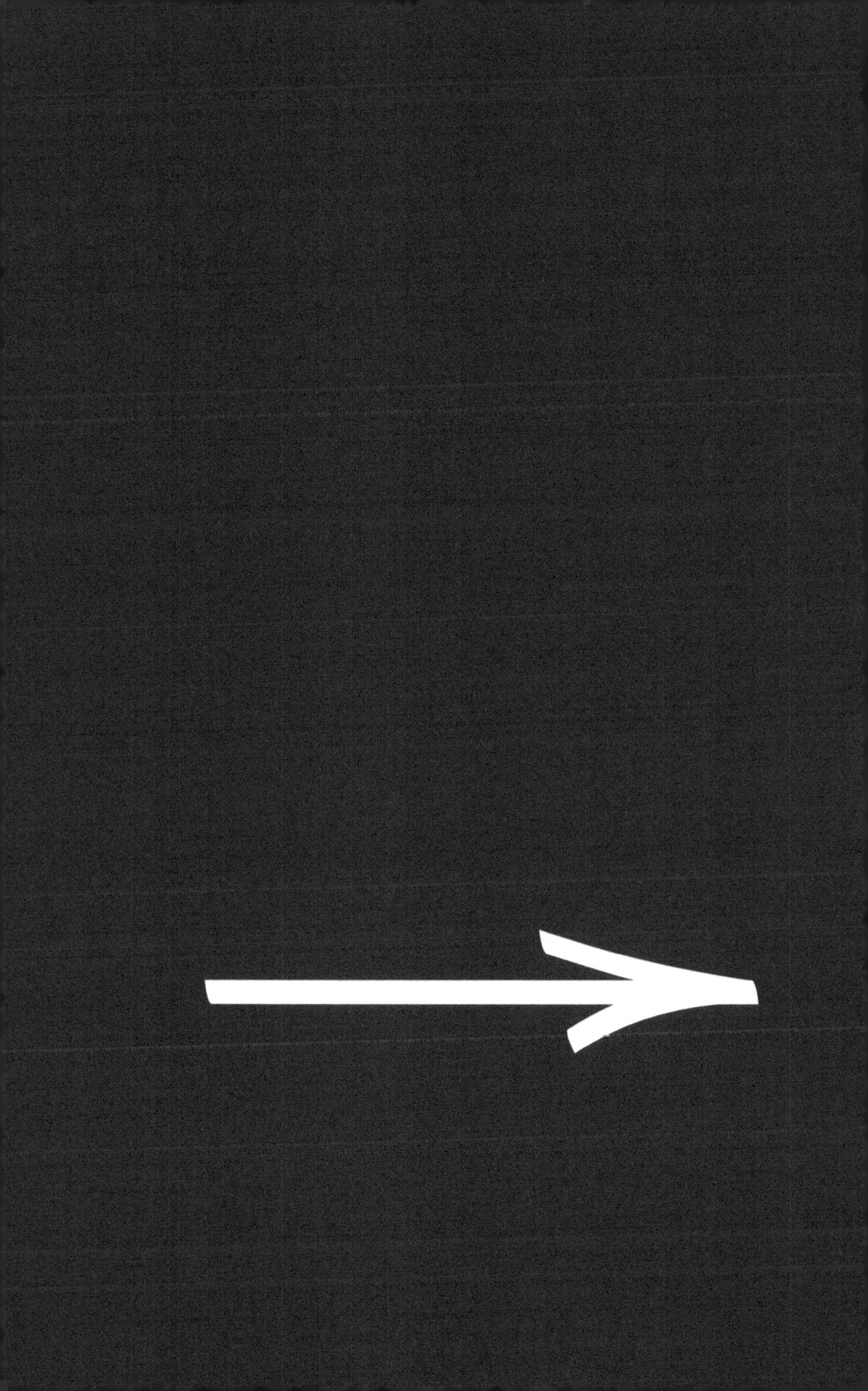

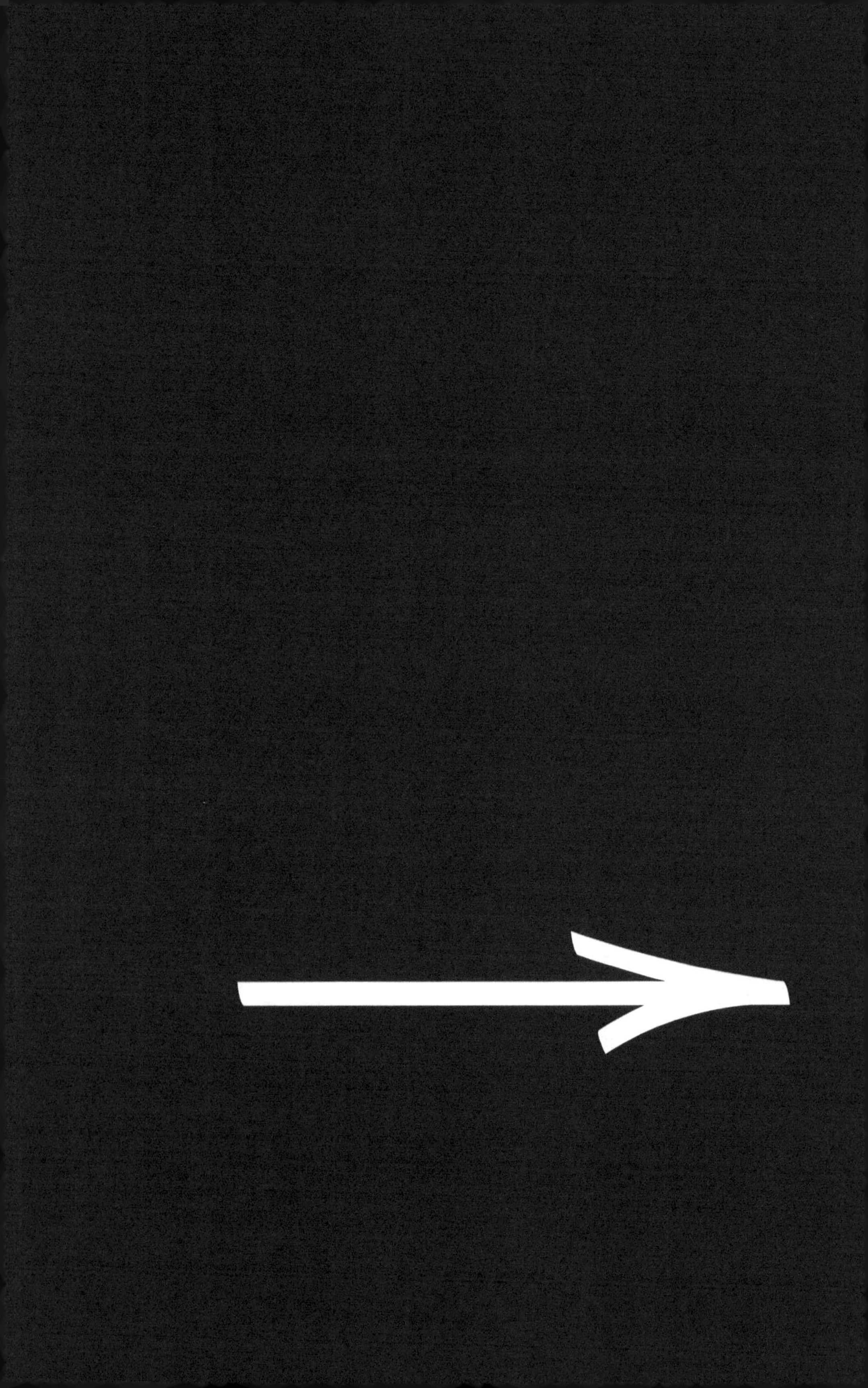

TECHNICAL AND THEORETICAL CONTENT

» THE AGILE MANIFESTO

In February 2001, in the US, 17 software developers started a movement that would later serve as a foundation for the creation of agile frameworks and methods. Dissatisfied with the results obtained in adopting existing methodologies, the group created a statement of values and principles that serve as a better way to develop software.

The *Agile Manifesto*[1] consists of a set of four values and twelve principles and represents the essence of Agile, meaning that these values and principles guide the options and alternatives related to practices, roles, ceremonies, methods, or frameworks.

Values

- » Individuals and interactions over processes and tools.
- » Working software over comprehensive documentation.
- » Customer collaboration over contract negotiation.
- » Responding to change over following a plan.

---

[1] Principles Behind The Agile Manifesto. Available at: https://agilemanifesto.org/principles.html. Accessed on: March, 2023.

Principles

1. Our highest priority is to satisfy the customer through early and continuous delivery of valuable software.

2. Welcome changing requirements, even late in development. Agile processes harness change for the customer's competitive advantage.

3. Deliver working software frequently, from a couple of weeks to a couple of months, with a preference to the shorter timescale.

4. Business people and developers must work together daily throughout the project.

5. Build projects around motivated individuals. Give them the environment and support they need, and trust them to get the job done.

6. The most efficient and effective method of conveying information to and within a development team is face-to-face conversation.

7. Working software is the primary measure of progress.

8. Agile processes promote sustainable development. The sponsors, developers, and users should be able to maintain a constant pace indefinitely.

9. Continuous attention to technical excellence and good design enhances agility.

10. Simplicity-the art of maximizing the amount of work not done-is essential.

11. The best architectures, requirements, and designs emerge from self-organizing teams.

12. At regular intervals, the team reflects on how to become more effective, then tunes and adjusts its behavior accordingly.

>> MINIMUM VIABLE PRODUCT (MVP)

MVP, short for Minimum Viable Product, is a concept that emerged in Silicon Valley and became very famous after the Lean Startup book[2] was published.

MVP avoids waste of time, money, and effort building a product that will not meet expectations. To mitigate these risks, you must understand and validate the assumptions about the business before trying to find a definitive solution.

This approach helps you validate and learn as quickly as possible. Unlike products created in the traditional way — long periods of prototype creation, analysis, and development — the MVP's goal is to validate a step of a product journey. In the case of software development, this refers to an initial set of features considered necessary in the short term. These features should deliver something useful to the users and contribute to learning about the business.

An example of MVP in the real world was the beginning of Zappos.[3] Its partners decided that, instead of spending months developing an e-commerce

---

2   The MVP, as the name implies, is the simplest set of features made available to users to validate an idea and collect essential data to guide the direction of the product. Even if the final product is something much bigger, this minimum is essential to find out if the path is correct or if it is necessary to change direction (pivot).

3   Caroli, Paulo. *MVP: How to Build the Minimum Viable Product.* Caroli.org, 20 July 2021. Available at: https://caroli.org/en/mvp-minimum-viable-product/#MVP-examples. Accessed on: March, 2023.

solution, they would just create a simplified web page for ordering shoes. They did not have any inventory. They took photos of the shoes from a nearby physical store. Once an online buyer made an order, they would purchase and ship the shoes to the buyers. With the MVP, they validated the fundamental business hypothesis and confirmed interest in the service. The result was a billionaire enterprise that started with minimum use of resources and reduced the associated risks.

Origin

The concept of MVP is originally linked to ideas popularized by the Toyota style of lean manufacturing.[4] Steve Blank,[5] an entrepreneur in Silicon Valley, created a defined methodology based on customer development. This was the beginning of the *Lean Startup* movement, which peaked with Eric Ries and the release of his book.[6]

Product increments

MVP does not mean that the product will not evolve and improve its features. Quite the contrary. The idea behind an MVP is to have a validated evolution guided by initial results, with correction or confirmation needed to guide further increments. These increments are added to the minimum product

---

4   Womack, James P.; Daniel T. Jones; Daniel Roos. *The machine that changed the world.* USA: Free Press, 2007.
    Ohno, Taiichi. *Toyota Production System.* USA: Productivity Press, 2019.
    Womack, James P.; Jones, Daniel T. *Lean thinking.* USA: Free Press, 2003.

5   Blank, Steve G. *The four steps to the epiphany,* 5th ed. New York: K & S Ranch, 2013.

6   Ries, Eric. *The Lean Startup: How Today's Entrepreneurs Use Continuous Innovation to Create Radically Successful Businesses.* Currency Publisher; 1st Edition, 2011.

already validated. They, in turn, are submitted to new checks on the direction of the product, now more elaborated and perhaps with a larger number of users (allowing to validate new, even more structured hypotheses).

It is very important to understand that MVP promotes evolutionary design. Therefore, the architecture, as well as the product construction tooling, should ideally also have this characteristic of gradual and continuous evolution.

In 2010, Jez Humble and David Farley published the book *Continuous Delivery*.[7] In it, they presented a fast, low-cost delivery process, enabling the incremental design of software products. This has been dubbed "continuous delivery" and encompasses the discipline of software development that promotes faster and more frequent deliveries. The essence behind the idea of "continuous delivery" is the same one that Eric Ries recommends for lean start-up: fast cycles to validate hypotheses.

Fast and frequent cycles allow for very short release times and low trial costs, which translates into critical success factors, especially for innovative or differentiating software products.

MVP Canvas

MVP Canvas is a tool to validate product ideas. It is a visual chart that helps align and define the MVP strategy. It helps teams avoid wasting time, money, and resources creating the wrong product. Startups and enterprises often go overboard when building a new product. They plan and add several features, thinking about the final result that, they believe, will meet the needs of their customers.

---

7 Humble, Jez; Farley, David. [*Continuous Delivery*]. Porto Alegre: Bookman, 2014.

The truth about almost all startups and new products is that nobody knows if they are going to work. If they knew what they were creating, then it wouldn't be a new product, but something that already exists.

So, we need to do what Facebook, Groupon, Airbnb, Spotify, Zappos, and many other successful companies did: adopt a new way to design and evolve products. The most efficient route to that target is to start by developing a minimum viable product, by using an MVP Canvas.

Validate the idea

It is impractical to design a feature for an MVP if you don't yet know how to describe what you expect as an outcome and how to measure it.

You must validate the business assumptions. Try to understand your users better. To do this, plan to collect MVP usage data that will help you verify the desired learning/result.

After defining the MVP, try to connect it to the expected outcomes and the business hypotheses. The following template helps with such a statement:

> We believe that _____________ (this MVP)
> will achieve _____________ (these expected outcomes).
> We will know that this happened based on _____________
> _____________ (metrics to validate business hypotheses).

It is important to fill in this type of template because if you can't complete it, you won't know what to expect from your MVP, or you won't know how to measure it. In either of these two scenarios, the product will be adrift and un-targeted.

The blocks on the MVP Canvas

The Canvas[8] has seven blocks that describe the points you need to discuss and define regarding your product's initial path: the MVP proposal, the expected outcome, the metrics to validate the hypothesis, the personas and their journeys, the features and the cost and schedule for their creation.

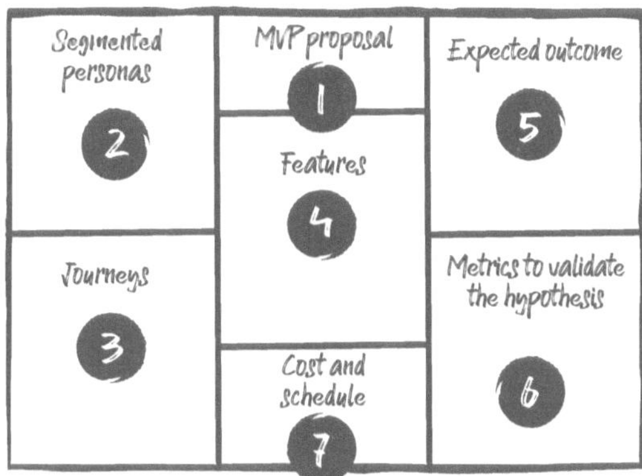

Here is the recommended order when filling it out or thinking about the blocks:

1. *MVP proposal* : What is the purpose of this MVP?

2. *Segmented personas*: Who is this MVP for? Can we segment and test it on a smaller group?

3. *Journeys*: What journeys are completed or enhanced by this MVP?

4. *Features*: What are we going to build in this MVP? What actions will be simplified or improved by it?

5. *Expected outcomes*: What lesson or result are we looking for in this MVP?

6. *Metrics to validate business hypotheses*: How can we measure the outcomes of this MVP?

---

7. *Cost and schedule*: What is the cost and expected delivery date of this MVP? Once delivered, how long will we need to collect the data to decide whether to move away or move forward?

The MVP Canvas is explained in detail in Paulo's book, *Lean Inception*.[9] The book explores the concept of MVP and describes how to effectively run a Lean Inception workshop to align a group of people on an MVP. The MVP Canvas is the final artifact created in a Lean Inception workshop.

---

9 Caroli, Paulo. *Lean Inception: How to Align People and Build the Right Product*. Rio de Janeiro: Editora Caroli, 2018.

>> LEAN INCEPTION

Lean Inception presents the complete step-by-step of a workshop that seeks to align people in order to build the right product. Let's look at how it works.

What is the purpose of a Lean Inception?

Agile engagements place an emphasis on early and continuous delivery of high-value software in line with business objectives and the needs of key users. Lean product development promotes the incremental release of the product starting via the minimum viable product (MVP), the simplest version of a product that can be made available to the business. But how can you plan the MVP and start the work as quickly as possible? How do you ensure the team starts the product design with a good initial alignment and an effective plan?

In a single week of collaborative work, the team will understand the product objectives, key users, and high-level functional scope so that the consulting engagement duration can be estimated and an incremental release strategy for the product can be identified.

During a Lean Inception, dynamic activities take place to define objectives, strategies, and product definition, as well as mapping and prioritizing the desirable features to be gradually delivered, in order to build each product increment. The main objective of the workshop is to make the team discover and collectively understand what will be developed. In the end, the team should be more aligned and should have a clearer vision of the way forward.

When should you do a Lean Inception?

You should schedule a Lean Inception if you are looking to align a team to build the right product. The most common reasons for scheduling a Lean Inception are:

- » Someone has invested in your startup and you're going to put your idea into action;
- » Your company is modernizing something and is going to redo an existing product;
- » A previous group failed to create the product, now there's a second attempt with more pressure and fewer resources;
- » Surveys indicate a good business direction, so the group is seeking a better product-market fit.[10]

Before starting out, the group should participate in a collaborative workshop with a sequence of activities that align and define objectives, strategies, and product scope. The optimal workshop uses Design Thinking[11] techniques paired with a Lean Startup approach.

---

10 Cagan, Marty. *Product Market Fit*, 2014. Available at: https://svpg.com/product-market-fit/. Accessed on: April 2021.

11 Schneider, Jakob; Stickdorn, Marc. *This is Service Design Thinking: basics, tools, cases.* Nova Jersey: Wiley, 2012.

How does it work?

Lean Inception works as a cookbook, presenting a sequence of quick and effective activities. These will allow the team to:

- Describe the product vision.
- Prioritize product objectives.
- Describe the main users, their personas, and their needs.
- Understand the main features.
- Understand the levels of uncertainty, effort, and business value of each feature.
- Describe the most important user journeys.
- Create an incremental product delivery plan, driven by the MVP concept.
- Apply various ice-breaking activities to make the inception environment more relaxed and fun.
- Calculate costs and estimate initial delivery dates and schedule.

Collaboration is the act of working together to perform a task and achieve common goals. The success of a Lean Inception is directly linked to the ability of the involved group to effectively collaborate in each of the above-mentioned activities as well as those described in the *Lean Inception* book.

A Lean Inception proposes a collaborative process of discovery and clarification in which the people involved work together in a sequence of activities to understand options and craft the MVP. The activities presented in the *Lean Inception* book represent structured methods of collaboration, seeking a creative environment with knowledge sharing, learning, and consensus building. The activities aim to increase the success of teams as they get involved in clarifying and resolving every step towards MVP.

What is the role of the facilitator?

All well-orchestrated workshops have two characteristics in common: they are well-structured and well-facilitated. The Lean Inception facilitator is a guide who encourages discussions during the workshop. To make this happen, the facilitator must possess a great deal of familiarity and experience with the format of the Lean Inception, its collaborative nature, and the sequence of activities that will be carried out.

However, the role of fostering the discussion does not imply that the facilitator is the main participant. Quite the contrary. The facilitator must be a mediator, one who facilitates the flow of ideas and active conversations among all the participants, who are the main interlocutors of the workshop. Consequently, the facilitator's job is to ensure that participants have responsibility, leadership, and collaboration throughout all planned activities. In other words, the facilitator's objective is to support the participants so that they can effectively participate in each activity and interaction planned for the workshop, dedicating themselves to the process and content, and ensuring that the latter is created in accordance with expectations and goals.

>> AN OVERVIEW OF KANBAN

Kanban is a method formulated by David J. Anderson[12] for managing the workflow of an incremental and evolutionary process. Influenced by Toyota's *just-in-time* model, the method is based on visualizing the workflow and based on that, acting on the process to avoid overloading the team members. Thanks to the visualization of work towards the value chain, the process, from its initial stage to the delivery, is exposed to the team members. Typically the value chain is represented on whiteboards with sticky notes or online tools. Work items are visually represented on these cards, commonly called kanban, the same name as the method (lower-k kanban is the card, while upper-k Kanban is the David Anderson method). Using the board makes it easier for the team to decide what to produce, when, and how much.

In software development, a small task typically takes hours and even days to complete. Additionally, you cannot see how many requirements are currently under review or how many requirements are currently being coded or tested. The fact is: we can't "see" the software-related work item and how it moves through the steps in the process until it's done. That is exactly how Kanban can help: by making those work items visible.

---

12 Anderson, David J. Kanban. Blue Hole Press Inc, 2013.

Visualize the workflow

The main idea of Kanban is to make the workflow visible to everyone, for example on a whiteboard or on the wall itself. Below is a representation of a kanban from a software development team.

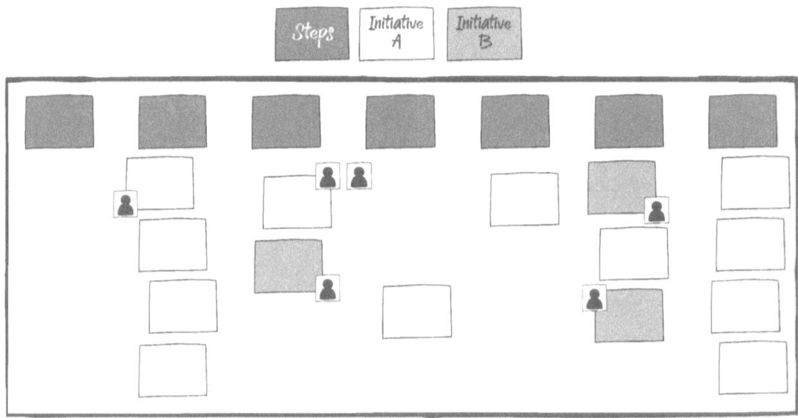

Since the wall is a two-dimensional surface, a kanban is presented in a tabular format, where work steps are columns, and work items, people's photos or avatars, and other design-related tags fill the space on the wall. These cards can be arranged in a horizontal line or not, it all depends on the team and how they represent and organize their work on the wall.

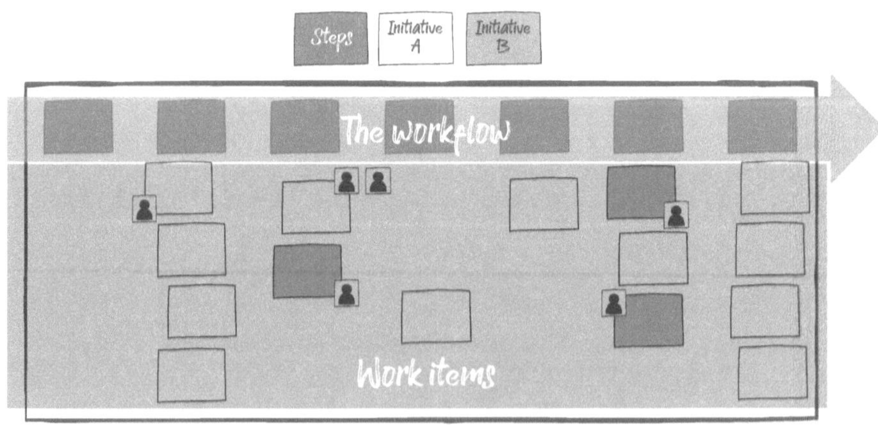

Limit the Work In Progress (WIP)

Limiting work-in-progress, or WIP, implies the kanban will follow a pull system. Work on each step of the process is limited so that a new task is only added/ "pulled" to the next step, when capacity is available within the WIP limit of that step. WIP restrictions identify bottlenecks and problem areas in the process, helping the team make decisions to resolve them. Limiting WIP is the main differentiator of the Kanban method: such a practice is what differentiates task boards (or visual boards, as they were known before David Anderson's Kanban method) and Kanban boards.

In the image above, numbers 3 and 1 represent, respectively, the WIP limit for the in dev step and the WIP limit for the testing step. In other words, the in dev step should have a maximum of three tasks at the same time, while the testing step should only have one.

Focus on the workflow

According to David Anderson, the main point of implementing a kanban is to create positive change. Before creating this change, the team has to know what to change. To do this, you should check how work items flow through the process and analyze possible problem areas that constrain the system. Thus, the team must implement changes in the work process to sort out such issues, identifying the problems and taking action to resolve them. This is all based on visualization of work and WIP limits. The goal is to always improve the work and the process in the continuous search for greater efficiency and effectiveness.

Driving continuous improvement

Kanban can be seen as a communication tool that quickly acquires and disseminates knowledge among team members. The main objective is to give all team members a shared view of the process and the current state of work. To that end, kanban delivers visual representations of the work steps, of the people, and the work itself.

But the Kanban method goes beyond that. From a simple approach — the visualization of the workflow and WIP limits — the team works within a strict system, which helps in identifying bottlenecks and acting on problem areas in the process. Thus, Kanban provides the team with a tool, a practice, and a process of continuous improvement.

>> AN OVERVIEW OF SCRUM

Scrum is an Agile[13] framework for developing, delivering, and sustaining complex products. Scrum was initially formalized for software development projects but has since then been applied to any scope of complex project and innovative work.

Scrum is especially suited for engagements with rapidly changing or highly emerging requirements. Software development with Scrum progresses through a series of iterations called Sprints, which typically last from one to four weeks.

Scrum meetings

The Scrum framework suggests that each Sprint starts with a planning meeting to define the work that must be done during the Sprint, and ends with a retrospective meeting, in which the team seeks continuous improvement regarding the process, delivery, and interaction between people.

---

13 *The Scrum Guide* (2018). Available at: https://www.scrumguides.org/scrum-guide.html. Accessed on: March 2020.

In addition to the planning and retrospective meetings, Scrum suggests two other events that should take place every Sprint:

>> The Sprint Review, where the team inspects the Sprint result and decides on future adaptations; and

>> The Daily Scrum, in which the team inspects progress toward the Sprint goal and adapts the Sprint backlog as needed. In this meeting, usually, all team members stand (so that the meeting doesn't take too long) and answer three questions, which help the team to self-organize, seeking daily alignment in relation to the work of the Sprint. The three questions are: What did I do yesterday? What am I going to do today? What, if anything, is blocking my progress?

In addition to the Scrum-suggested meetings, many teams also hold backlog refinement meetings during the Sprint. In these meetings, the product backlog is revisited to seek further understanding (and refinement) of upcoming requirements, which will be candidates for the next Sprint.

The Sprint

Sprints promote a cadence, typically one to four weeks, depending on the team preference. This cadence allows for predictability, ensuring inspection and adaptation of progress.

In the Scrum agile world, we avoid complete and detailed descriptions of how everything should be done in a Sprint. That's because the team will know the best way to solve the problem at hand.

That's why the Sprint Planning meeting is described in terms of the goals and desired outcome. The desired result is a commitment to a set of features or stories to be developed in the next Sprint, thus seeking a balance between autonomy, flexibility, and team commitment. Such commitment is revisited in the review meeting.

All the work necessary to achieve the product objective is carried out by the team during the Sprints, including other events: Sprint Planning, Daily Scrum, Sprint Review, and Retrospective. During the course of a Sprint, no changes should occur that could jeopardize the Sprint goal.

Scrum roles

Scrum fosters a cross-functional and self-organizing team. The effectiveness of the team depends on the members' ability to work together and make the best use of each individual's skills. That's what makes the team cross-functional. The Scrum team is self-organized. There should not be a need for a team leader who decides who will do what task and how. Tasks and issues should be raised by everyone.

Despite being self-organized, Scrum teams still need people to fill three specific roles:

The Scrum Master

The first is the role of the Scrum Master (SM), someone who is experienced with the framework and who has the responsibility to ensure that the Scrum framework is understood and applied. Their main objective is to maximize the team's efficiency. The best Scrum Masters are the kind of people who feel more satisfaction in facilitating the success of others than their own. A person in the Scrum Master role must feel comfortable and secure with the framework to the point of giving all control over the product to the Product Owner (PO), and also all control over software development to the team.

The Product Owner (PO)

The second specific role is the Product Owner (PO). This person represents the business, customers, or users, and guides the team toward building the right product. The main function of the PO is to prioritize the backlog based on the alignment between stakeholders, both internal and external to the Scrum team. The PO maximizes value through an ongoing product development process, guided by learning and experimentation, and leads the development effort through clarifications and prioritization of the work. As such, the PO must be available to the team to answer questions and direct the team at every moment or inquiry.

This combination of authority and availability to the development team makes the role of PO a key part of the framework. Since Scrum values the team's self-organization and autonomy, the PO must respect the direction and ability of the team to create its own action plan.

Developers

All the other people on the Scrum team are considered developers, this being the third role of Scrum. These are the people with different skill sets who are committed to creating any and all product increments.

Scrum artifacts

Scrum has three artifacts: the product backlog, the Sprint backlog, and the product increment. They share the same objective: to maximize transparency and promote alignment about the work.

The product backlog and the Sprint backlog describe the work to be done, for the product and for the Sprint, respectively. The increment is a piece of the product to be developed. Each increment is added to the increments previously delivered. Multiple increments can be created in a Sprint. To provide value, each and every increment must be usable.

Teamwork, cadence, and clarity

The Scrum team members (Scrum Master, PO, and developers, with their varied backgrounds) actively participate in all meetings with a high level of autonomy, transparency, and commitment. In the Sprint Planning meeting, the team decides on the Sprint backlog, which is tracked daily and re-evaluated in the review meeting. Through the pursuit of continuous improvement (the main objective of the retrospective meeting), the Scrum team typically achieves high levels of performance. Much of this is achieved through teamwork, alignment during the Sprints, and the clarity of each role and each meeting.

FEATURES AND USER STORIES: INVEST

Features are typically described on a higher level than user stories. Therefore, before starting to work on a feature, it must be analyzed and detailed into its respective stories.

Feature is the description of a user's action or interaction with the product. For example: "print invoice," "consult a detailed statement," or "invite Facebook friends." The description of a feature should be as simple as possible. The user is trying to do something. The product must have a feature for this, and should solve the question, "What is this user trying to do?"

Typically, development teams work with user stories, and part of the clarification of a user story involves drilling down a little more and applying feature mapping to stories.

The user story is presented in a textual format to deliver a concise description of a requirement that seeks to answer three basic questions: who, what, and why. Typically, an MVP has one or more features that translate into some user stories in the following format:

- » *As a* __________ (persona/profile)
- » *I want* __________ (action to be performed/step towards accomplishing something)
- » *So that* __________ (value for the business and/or for the user)

Bill Wake, in his book *Extreme Programming Explored*,[14] created the acronym INVEST, which defines a simple set of rules used in the proper creation of user stories. Each letter of the acronym represents one of the six important characteristics of a user story: independent, negotiable, valuable, estimable, small, and testable.

A few years after the acronym creation, Mike Cohn,[15] renamed the letter S from *small* to *sized appropriately*, reflecting that some people created stories that were a little larger, but adequate to its context.

>> *Independent*: One story does not depend on another.

>> *Negotiable*: A story captures the essence of what is desired. It is not a closed contract. Conversations and negotiations are welcome.

>> *Valuable*: A story clearly describes customer value.

>> *Estimable*: A story provides enough information for the team to make a high-level estimate.

>> *Small/Sized appropriately*: A good story should be relatively small in size to be completed in the shortest possible time and fit into an iteration, considering the context of the team.

>> *Testable*: A story must be clear enough that tests can be defined for it.

---

14 Wake, William C. ; *Extreme Programming Explored*. Boston: Addison-Wesley Professional, 2001.

15 Cohn, Mike; *User stories applied*. Boston: Addison-Wesley Professional, 2004.

» FEATURES AND USER STORIES: THE 3C'S

In addition to INVEST, a good user story consists of three elements, commonly called 3C's:

- » *Card*: The description of a user story must fit on an index card, containing enough information to identify it. The most common format is:

  As a ____

  I want ____

  So that ____

- » *Conversation*: The main intention of putting user stories in an index card format is the limited space for writing. Therefore, a lot of conversation is needed to clarify doubts and detail the work needed to implement them. Working with user stories means accepting that conversations about the work will be ongoing, not just at the beginning when the requirement is initially defined.

- » *Confirmation*: This is where we determine if the objective of the user's story is achieved. To do this, the acceptance criteria confirm that the user story has been implemented correctly and successfully delivered. Acceptance criteria must be defined for each story before the team starts to implement it, so there are no surprises when reviewing the story.

User stories have three critical aspects: the story card must follow a simple template (As a... I want... So that). From that, we will have collaborative conversations to better understand and detail the story, until, when ready, we will receive confirmation, usually from the Product Owner (PO).

Acceptance criteria

Acceptance criteria is a textual format that describes how to test a feature. Typically a user story will have some acceptance criteria (or ACs).

>> *Given* _______________________ (initial scenario)

>> *When* _______________________ (action taken)

>> *Then* _______________________ (expected state)

ACs set the boundaries for a user story. Once the PO confirms they are fulfilled, everyone involved will know the story is complete.

Tasks

It is very common to break a story into even smaller pieces of the work that must be done. These are tasks. By listing the tasks needed to build a story, the development team goes into the technical details of how the smaller pieces will be implemented. Unlike stories, tasks do not follow a defined textual format. They are more straightforward, with very technical language, from the development team to the development team.

A task identifies something that needs to be done, something necessary for a story. As such, the task will not necessarily be self-contained and will not demonstrate business value. Most of them tend to be for developers, described in terms used by them. Some examples of tasks are:

> Change table fields.

> Create test accounts for users.

> Automate data generation scripts, and so on.

An example

Below is an example of a feature that has been split into three stories, with some acceptance criteria and tasks.

Feature: find football (soccer) matches available without geolocation

Story 1

> As an unregistered player,

> I want to see matches near an address I have entered

> so that I can find a match near my current location.

Story 2

> As a registered player,

> I want to check matches near my home

> so that I can find a match near my home.

Story 3

> As a registered player,

> I want to search for matches close to my work

> so that I can find a match near my workplace.

Story 3: Acceptance criteria (Example 1)

> Given there is a match that is less than 10 kilometers from my work,

> when I look for a match close to my workplace

> (then) I find a match.

Story 3: Acceptance criteria (Example 2)

> Given there are no matches within 10 kilometers of my work,

> when I look for a match close to my workplace

> (then) I do not find any matches.

Story 3: Tasks

> Create UI to show matches near the workplace (with data hardcoded).

> Create backend logic to search by proximity (10 km hardcoded).

> Change hardcoded parameter to configuration field.

> Create test data to search for match near the workplace.

> Change DB to include work address.

>> THE SPOTIFY MODEL

The Spotify model is the name given to a type of product team structure. Spotify is a product company, famous for its music streaming app. In 2012, the company was growing rapidly, with thirty product teams spread across three cities.

That year, Henrik Kniberg and Anders Ivarsson published an article, *Scaling Agile @ Spotify with Tribes, Squads, Chapters & Guilds*[16] proposing how to deal with multiple teams in a product organization. This proposal became known as the Spotify model.

The model is summarized by the following image, which demonstrates the following points:

>> A tribe is made up of teams that work in related areas (*e.g.* backend infrastructure tribe).

>> A squad is similar to a Scrum team, a cross-functional team with experts in a product area (*e.g.* Advanced Indexing squad).

>> A chapter is formed by people in the same role (*e.g.* web developers' chapter).

>> A guild is a community of interest, made up of people from different roles (*e.g.* agile coaching guild).

---

16 *Spotify Scaling. Available at: https://blog.crisp.se/wp-content/uploads/2012/11/SpotifyScaling.pdf. Accessed on: March 2020.*

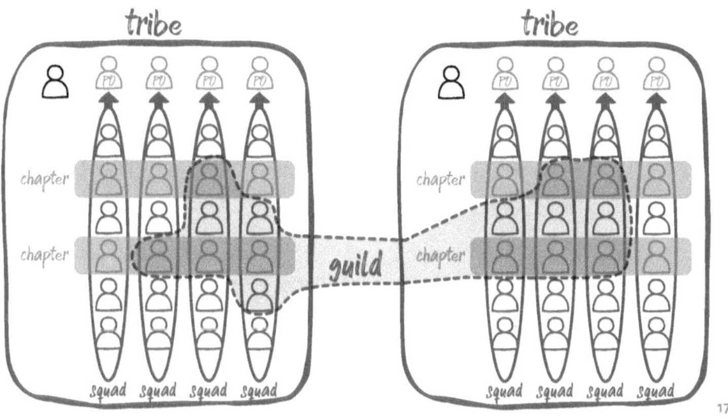

17 Original image available at: http://kasburger.blogspot.com.br/2017/01/agile-tribe-leader-is-spider-in-web-of.html. Accessed on: March 2020.

OBJECTIVES AND KEY RESULTS (OKR)

Objectives and Key Results (OKR) is a goal-setting framework created by Intel in the 1970s that is used very successfully by Silicon Valley investors from large companies such as Google,[18] Oracle, Twitter, LinkedIn, and Dropbox. Currently, OKRs are being applied all over the world, from startups to large organizations.

The main idea of OKRs is for the organization to define a set of cascading goals. For example, OKRs must first be defined for the organization. OKRs are then defined for departments and business units and then for teams. And so on, cascading down to the individuals, setting up their own OKRs. Each entity (organization, department, individual) should have four to six objectives and up to five key results per objective.

The following is a model for OKRs shared by Felipe Castro.[19] Felipe explains that an OKR has two components, the objective (what we want to achieve) and a set of key results (how we know if we are getting there).

---

18 Yarow, Jay. *This Is The Internal Grading System Google Uses For Its Employees — And You Should Use It Too.* Available at: http://www.businessinsider.com/googles-rankin- g-system-okr-2014-1. Accessed on: March 2020.

19 Castro, Felipe. "The Silicon Valley way of setting goals: an introduction to OKR." Available at: https://medium.com/the-alignment-shop/introduction-to-okr-9912085830f0. Accessed on: March 2020.

We will _________________________ (objective) ________________ ,

as measured by _____________ (this set of key results) _________ .

The objective can be qualitative, while the key results must be quantitative. The objective sets a goal for a defined period of time, usually a quarter. Key results indicate whether the goal has been achieved by the end of the time.

OKR – Example

Here is an example by Felipe Castro of an OKR from a technology company that wants to increase customer engagement and satisfaction.

Objective:

Delight our customers.

Key results:

> Recurring visits: Average of 3.3 visits per week per active user.

> Achieve NPS (net promoter score) of 90.

> Unpaid traffic (organic) of 80%.

> Engagement: 75% of users fill out a complete profile.

» SOME SPECIFIC PRACTICES

The practices described below were used in the team's daily routine. They will appear later in the book and are better explained in this section as well.

Daily Scrum style

Every day the team following Scrum holds a meeting to check the progress of the work items. That meeting is the Daily Scrum.

Traditional Daily Scrum or Daily Round-Robin

While standing, the team answers the three questions listed below. They help the team to organize itself, seeking daily alignment in relation to the Sprint work:

- » What did I do yesterday?
- » What am I going to do today?
- » What, if anything, is blocking my progress?

We call this meeting the traditional Daily Scrum or Daily Round-Robin.[20] Round-Robin is the algorithm that assigns time fractions to each process in

---

20 Round-Robin. Available at: https://pt.wikipedia.org/wiki/Round-robin. Accessed on: March 2020.

equal parts and in a circular fashion. And that's how traditional Daily Scrums are: the team forms a circle, and each person has a fraction of the time to answer those three questions.

Top-to-bottom

Many teams make their work (tasks, stories, or other work items) visible via a top-down list of work items represented on a visual board (the doing/in progress column on the board for example).

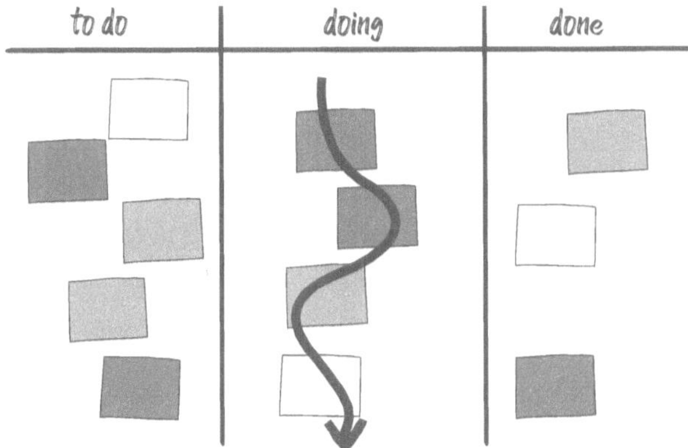

These visual boards can have various names (including brand names of online tools). The most common are kanban, task board, Scrum board, Trello, and Jira. In the top-to-bottom Daily Scrum, the team follows the board talking about each item that is in progress, from top to bottom. In this style, the three Daily Scrum questions should be:

- » What did we do on this item yesterday?
- » What are we going to do on this item today?
- » What, if anything, is blocking progress on this item?

The person responsible for the work item is usually identified on the board. In this case, that person updates the task, and the Daily Scrum continues with the next work item in a top-to-bottom order.

What is the current style of your Daily Scrum?

It is very common for a new team to adopt one of these two styles. And it also happens that, from time to time, the team will change it.

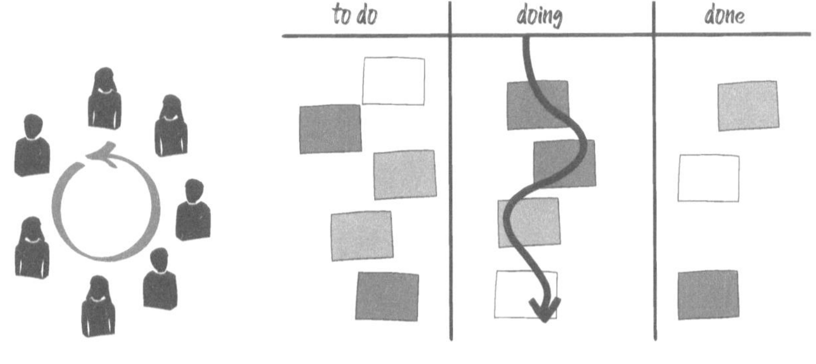

Daily Scrum Round-robin   Daily Scrum Top Down

Planning a retrospective

The retrospective is a one-hour meeting (approximately) that takes place frequently (usually once a week or once per Sprint for Scrum teams) in which people on the team talk about what went well during the period, what can be improved, and what they should do to improve.

Retrospectives are essential to unite the team in a common goal and to prevent misunderstandings from escalating to levels of interpersonal discomfort, which, in turn, can lead to reduced communication and group disruption. It also creates the environment for people to reflect and listen to how everyone is feeling, to talk about a specific topic (related to the context and team situation), and to pursue Kaizen — continuous improvement.

Here are some questions you should answer when planning your retrospective:

> *Moment in time:* Where are you on the timeline? Are you establishing a new team? Are you trying to learn from the past? Are you preparing for an upcoming release?

> *Context:* What are you looking for? Are you looking to focus on action items? Do you need to boost team morale? Do you want to measure team happiness?

Based on these factors, you need to choose which activity (or sequence of activities) is most appropriate.

In addition to thinking of the retrospective that is appropriate for the team's context and time, many teams have the retrospective as a recurring meeting. That's why they look for alternatives to avoid monotony caused by always following the same format, with the same activities. By varying the retrospective format and activities, the team can look at different angles and perspectives, generating new insights.

A seven-step agenda for effective retrospectives is suggested in the *Fun-Retrospectives*[21] book and website. Throughout this book, you will find some of these retrospectives.

---

21 Caroli, Paulo; Caetano, Tainã. *FunRetrospectives: Activities and Ideas for Making Agile Retrospectives More Engaging.* Rio de Janeiro: Editora Caroli, 2020. You can also access the website available at: www.FunRetrospectives.com/ .

1. Context

Why are we running this retrospective? What will it cover?

Retrospectives, like any other meeting, are most effective if participants align their expectations before joining. You can start with a pre-defined context or set it in real-time with the participants. But it should be clear to everyone what the context of the retrospective is.

2. Prime directive

In *Project Retrospectives: A Handbook for Team Reviews*,[22] Norman Kerth and Gerald Weinberg present the prime directive for retrospectives, a statement designed to set the stage for the retrospective:

> Regardless of what we discover, we understand and truly believe that everyone did the best job they could, given what they knew at the time, their skills and abilities, the resources available, and the situation at hand.

The Prime directive is essential in setting the tone for the meeting. Make it visible to all participants and read it aloud at the beginning of your retrospective.

Is this really a retrospective meeting? Is the team looking back? Caroli and Tainã, authors of the book *FunRetrospectives*, recognized that some "retrospectives" were not about the past, but about team building or a future

---

[22] Weinberg, Gerald; Norman, Kerth; *Project Retrospectives.* Boston: Addison-Wesley Professional, 2013.

perspective. So they created and made available two other prime directives, respectively for team building and futurespectives.

> Cooperation is the act of working with others and acting together to accomplish a job. A team is a partnership of unique people who bring out the very best in each other, and who know that even though they are wonderful as individuals, they are even better together. Coming together is a beginning; staying together is progress; working together is success.

> Hope and confidence come from proper involvement and a willingness to predict the unpredictable. We will fully engage in this opportunity to unite around an inclusive vision and join hands in constructing a shared future.

3. Energizer

Energizing activities, or icebreakers, are simple and quick to warm up the team and promote group interaction. These activities help to create a friendly environment and make people more comfortable participating in other activities. They are essential to create a lighter and more fun atmosphere (retrospectives don't have to and shouldn't be heavy and boring meetings!).

Examples of activities: *Ping Pong* and *Isn't That Crazy.*

4. Check-in

Check-ins are short activities; think of them as an appetizer to whet everyone's appetite for the main course and at the same time provide the facilitator with feedback on participants' involvement.

Examples of activities: *Safety Check* and *One Word.*

5. Main course

The main course is the main activity of a retrospective meeting that seeks to promote continuous improvement. This is where you collect data, check team morale, talk about positive things, appreciate people, and seek improvement. Choose the main course for the moment and the context in question. This is the main activity of your meeting; the information you gather and discuss will set the tone for continuous improvement.

Examples of activities: *Timeline with Ups and Downs* and *Small Starfish.*

6. Filtering

After the main course, you may have a lot of material in front of you. It is important to have well-defined criteria to decide what will be discussed. In the limited time of the meeting, you may have to leave some topics out. If this is the case, define the filtering criteria with your team.

Examples of filters: *Groups with the highest number* and *Voting.*

7. Checkout

The meeting is almost over, and you need to close it. Check-out activities help with the closing process. These are very short activities. Think of them as an effective hotel checkout, where the guest (participant) quickly exits with the feeling of being heard and giving valuable feedback to the hotel. The participant can even carry a note or action item in their bag.

Examples of activities: *What-Who-When* and *Personal Note*.

All examples listed above are in the chapter "Retrospective activities" in the Appendix section.

Confidence voting

This is a practice used to give visibility to how confident a team is about something that is being proposed, such as achieving the Sprint goal. In addition to preventing individuals from being influenced by others, it also works as a safety check and helps to highlight when something isn't right and needs to be adjusted before the team can move forward.

This practice consists of asking everyone on the team to simultaneously show a number (using their fingers) that represents their confidence level between 0 and 5.

5: I am completely sure I can do this.

4: I can't think of any problems right now, I believe I can do it.

3: There are few risks with low probability and/or impact. It's doable.

2: I have some concerns but I'm willing to give it a try.

1: I have great concerns about what is being proposed. I can accept the team's decision, but I need more information to feel confident.

0: I don't feel confident at all, and I wouldn't want to go ahead with it.

It is important that a conversation takes place if someone has voted 0 or 1, or if the majority of votes are below 3. In these scenarios, information, knowledge, or resources (such as time) are possibly lacking, preventing the team from doing what is being proposed. The conversation will aim to provide information or guarantee that the necessary knowledge and resources will be available to the team. If this is not possible, the proposal should be revised so that the team feels confident and can commit.

TDD

TDD (Test-driven development) is a form of software development in which development is guided by tests, as the name implies. TDD is one of the practices of eXtreme Programming (XP), method and book written by Kent Beck, published in 1999.[23] TDD is based on repeating a short cycle: code the test, code the functional code to make the test pass, improve the code. This way of working encourages a simpler design and inspires confidence to add, modify or improve the code.

---

23 Beck, Kent. *eXtreme Programming Explained.* Boston: Addison-Wesley Professional, 1999.

>> DEVOPS ASSESSMENT

The assessment presented here is based on the version published in the *InfoQ Brasil*[24] article written by Bruno Tavares and Paulo Caroli, which was inspired by the book *Continuous Delivery* by Jez Humble and David Farley. It should be noted that the greatest benefit of applying such an assessment lies in the conversations and advice given by people with a lot of practical and theoretical experience in DevOps.

> Continuous delivery provides a standard language for the activities of building, testing, and deploying software on the production path. In addition, it refers to Continuous Integration as a starting point, but extending it to meet the needs of the business as a whole, providing a continuous cycle of software releases.

The DevOps assessment is a conversation based on a series of questions that help to visually identify eight maturity domains in the (ongoing) team delivery process in an organization:

---

24 Tavares, Bruno; Caroli, Paulo. [How to Assess (and Assist) Your Team with Continuous Delivery]. Available at: https://www.infoq.com/br/articles/como-avaliar-sua-equipe-com-entrega-continua. Accessed on: March 2020.

1. Delivery process.
2. Quality control.
3. Configuration management.
4. Environments and deployments.
5. Data storage.
6. Technical architecture.
7. Organizational alignment.
8. Visibility.

Delivery process

This is the ability to build and test a product release base to ensure individual changes are compatible with other changes made, synchronously and continuously. This allows the team to manage the pace of their work and to deliver a high-quality, reproducible product on demand.

Reference - Score 0

> The discovery of errors made due to incompatibility of changes occur in production.

> There are no guidelines or practices for verifying compatibility between parts of the system.

Reference - Score 3

> Managed and reproducible practice is applied consistently (both manually and automatically), using defined standards and practices, which everyone understands.

> The team is expected to operate in a consistent and predictable manner, but the metrics focus on failure rather than success.

Reference - Score 5

> Each successful build generates a release candidate.
> The focus is on making more frequent commits, with increasing confidence in the product's quality.
> CI[25] (continuous integration) creates environments to allow scalability of tests.
> Tests are run in parallel or on multiple machines.
> Delivery pipeline extends to production.

Quality control

Quality control is the concept of systematically and quickly discovering problems during the product delivery process with more frequent and shorter feedback loops to guarantee quality. Discovering defects earlier in the development cycle is less costly and easier to fix. Problems are not exposed to the user because they are identified and resolved before reaching production.

Reference - Score 0

> There are no testers.
> The product is delivered directly to production untested.
> Customer support deals with defects.

---

25 Fowler, Martin. Continuous Integration, 2006. Available at: https://www.martinfowler.com/articles/continuousIntegration.html. Accessed on: April 2021.

Reference - Score 3

> Developing and testing are collaborative functions.

> Testing is part of everyone's responsibility on the delivery team.

> Awareness to build with quality instead of reacting when finding something broken.

> Automation is in place, but not comprehensively or sustainably.

> The practices are planned to shorten the feedback loops and move the tests to the beginning of the cycle.

Reference - Score 5

> "Immune" production systems detect implementation failures and automatically correct them.

> The team has a high awareness of testing practices and selects those that provide the greatest benefit to the product as well as a rapid response to change.

> New methodologies, techniques and approaches are explored and applied to improve product quality.

> Approximately 100% test coverage.

Configuration management

Ability to track changes made to artifacts that affect the behavior of a system and manage multiple contributions to a single artifact. This includes source code, libraries, configuration files, tests, environment descriptions, dependent libraries, database structure, supporting documentation, and anything else related to product delivery.

Reference - Score 0

> Changes are made by multiple team members simultaneously, without any effort to maintain versions or track who made the change and when.

> If version control exists, it is usually done by individuals who need structure to organize their activities.

> There are no means for a team to revert changes to a previous working version.

Reference - Score 3

> The items needed to configure all environments are identified.

> A single set of tools for product configuration management has been determined and there is an effort to move all delivery artifacts to the version control system.

> Test scripts, libraries, and dependencies are managed.

> All team members commit frequently and regularly.

Reference - Score 5

> There is a single flow of contribution for everyone involved, which is constantly validated through deliverables.

> The team changes practices and adjust artifacts frequently as the product evolves.

> New version control tools are evaluated and implemented to meet the evolving needs of product delivery practices.

> Development is all done on the main branch and the team is able to deliver and add new features without resorting to long-lived branches.

Environments and deployments

This represents the availability of suitable environments for development and testing to ensure that the product will function as expected in production. The ability to go into production with minimal work and no disruption to operations and end users.

Reference – Score 0

> There are no separate environments for development and testing.

> Development environments are overcrowded.

> Firewalls and network configurations are often blockers to development.

Reference – Score 3

> Automated provisioning with scripted deployments.

> There is still reliance on individual skills to ensure the deployment will work in production.

> Test environments are readily available and reproducible with manual work and coordination across operational teams.

Reference – Score 5

> There is pipeline capacity for continuous delivery.

> Environments are easily replicated on-demand as needed using a self-service model to facilitate the optimal feedback loop.

> Provisioning and configuration of the environment are fully automated, preferably using a cloud-based system.

> Environments are regularly reviewed to simplify and optimize the effective use of technology.

> Provisioning is scalable to meet fluctuating demands.

Data storage

This is the ability for everyone to follow the changes made to the database structure for every release and also the effect that these changes bring. This includes the ability to roll forward or rollback the version of all changes. Database changes must be scripted alongside other deployment artifacts, and reusable test data must be created for all environments.

Reference - Score 0

> The development team is unaware of the process and functioning of the database.

> Complete control of data and database is carried out by an external team.

Reference - Score 3

> Database changes are performed automatically as part of the delivery process.

> Datasets are defined for different purposes in the delivery process. For example: development environment, integration, user acceptance testing (UAT), load, and performance.

> All datasets are scripted and included in the delivery pipeline.

Reference - Score 5

> Automatic feedback loops for the database performance and delivery is present in the process and it is used to drive improvements.

> Testing is performed using isolated datasets that are well sized for the purpose of testing (pre-production environments use smaller datasets).

Technical architecture

Holistic thinking about technical decisions and their effects on the business' ability to change. This is expensive and difficult to change once the technology is in use. The concept refers to the mechanisms in place for making architectural decisions as well as decisions around shared resources. Designing components around business capabilities to reduce costs and risks and facilitate changes.

Reference - Score 0

> Technical decisions are made on the spot and there is no long-term vision or technical planning.

> Use of high-level components and business logic in parts that are difficult to test.

> Dependencies are not managed and not fully understood.

> Dependencies are not around business capabilities.

> Dependency versioning is poorly managed.

> Code does not have automated testing and the architecture does not allow for automated unit testing.

> Architecture only allows big bang releases.

Reference - Score 3

> There are open lines of communication between architects and product teams.

> Product teams participate in design decisions.

> Communication between the team and the architect is informal and frequent.

> Teams use modern practices to isolate features/services to gain ability to deliver independently.
> Teams are mature enough to decide when to refactor and architect the system to support new features or dependencies.
> There is a versioning strategy for dependencies and how to handle changes that break the API design, but it is not always followed.

Reference - Score 5

> Mechanisms exist to enable the product team to make architectural and technology decisions. That's because the technical vision is clear and transparent.
> Architects are fully engaged with the business to enable business innovation.
> The architecture allows you to measure and tune to improve performance.
> The architecture can scale in a variety of ways, depending on the business needs.
> The team is able to make changes in the build process, pipeline, and delivery stages during the architecture lifecycle, to optimize both the whole and local areas.
> API design versioning strategies are well understood and managed by all teams.

Organizational alignment

The ability of team members to share ideas and work together to improve processes and the product, delivering working software faster and more securely. Team's ability to share knowledge and skills and determine improvements.

Reference – Score 0

> No effort to facilitate open and transparent communication.

> Large teams of individuals performing tasks in isolation.

> The technical manager is only a nominal position.

> Code sections are entirely owned by individuals.

Reference – Score 3

> All functional teams are seen as members of the product team and are represented in regular product meetings aimed at improving delivery.

> Operations teams provide an advisory service to product teams.

> Sharing knowledge among cross-functional groups is not a common and consistent practice.

> There is a plan to maintain continuity of team composition between interactions.

Reference – Score 5

> The business's ability to submit changes is the factor that limits what the product team is working on.

> Companies have rich data based on usage patterns and the ability to release new products to select end-users in production (canary release, A/B testing, etc.).

> All team members are qualified in all technical areas and there is little specialization reliant on single individuals.

Visibility

The ability to plan and respond to the Product Owner's change requests in a way that allows for a consistent and predictable pace of work that is also completely transparent to everyone.

Reference – Score 0

> There is no easy tool or way to check what was done, by whom and why.

Reference – Score 3

> All product changes can be tracked through a common tool, shared across teams, which includes tracking approvals and test results.
> Failures can easily be linked to individual changes early in the lifecycle.

Reference – Score 5

> There is complete transparency of what is part of each release.
> The PO is able to determine when a version goes into production and is no longer dependent on the team's ability to deliver.
> Control evidence and decisions made can be generated through automated toolsets used by the product team.

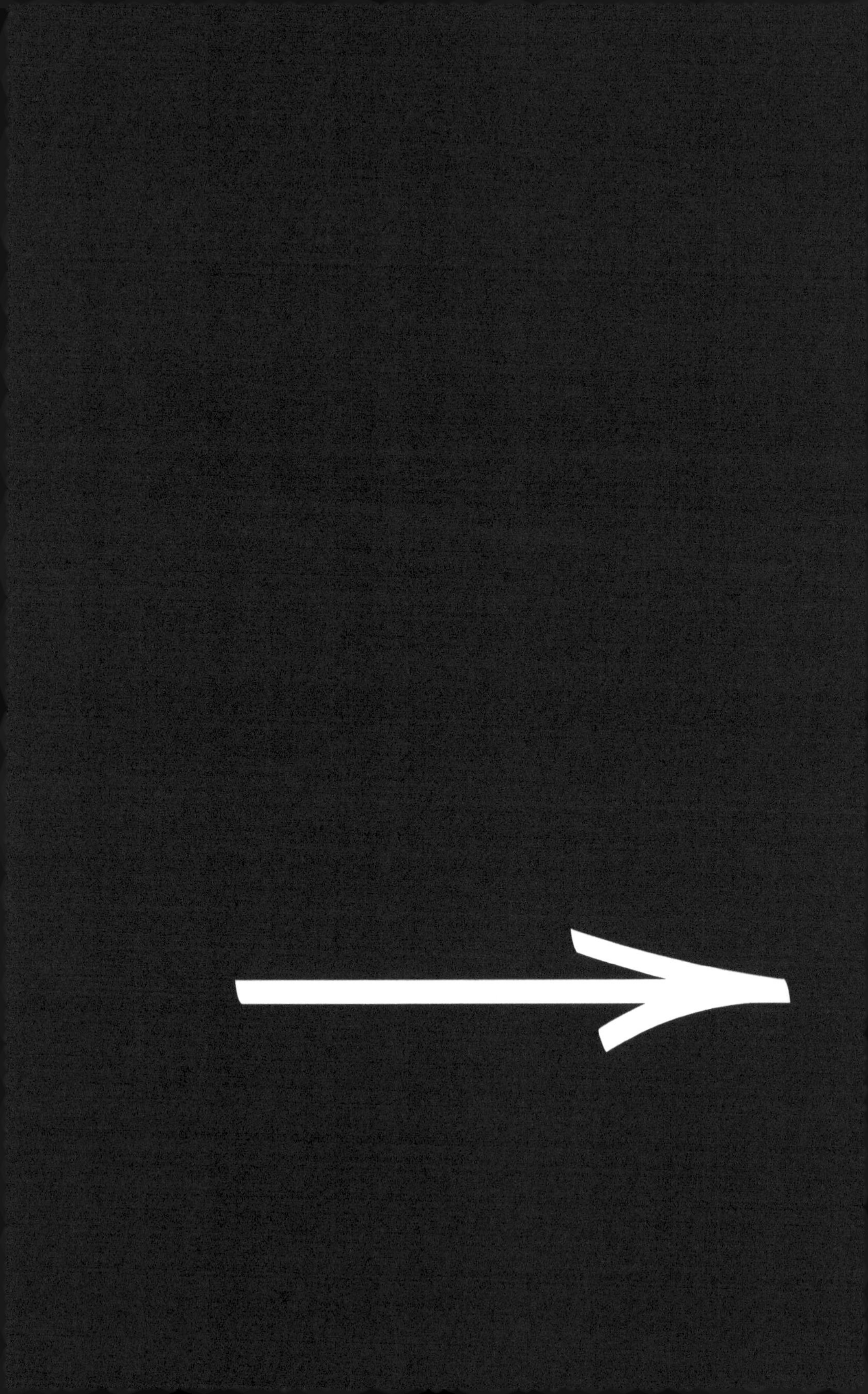

THE DAY-TO-DAY OF A TEAM IN ACTION

>> PLANNING THE WORK

The Agile consultant's work is organized into six weeks of work with specific deliverables, each of which has a distinct focus. The intention is for the Agile consultant to work with the team only for this period and, at the end, present a report with recommendations and next steps.

The team was chosen as an example among several other teams in the organization that work in a similar way. The main objectives of this work are: 1. to help the team; and 2. share recommendations so they can be applied to more teams in the organization.

WEEK 1: Lean Inception

Tasks:

> Facilitate the team's Lean Inception.

> Align on MVP and delivery plan.

> Conduct meetings with stakeholders.

Deliverables:

> Product roadmap (on a slide).

> Work plan for agile consulting.

WEEK 2: Team agreements

Tasks:

> Follow up on team meetings.

> Align on how the work will be performed.

Deliverables:

> Presentation showing how the team works.

> Visual print-out on the ways of working (document to be placed on the wall that demonstrates how the team works, including main team meetings and ceremonies).

WEEK 3: Technical excellence

Tasks:

> Follow up on architecture meetings.

> Apply the DevOps assessment.

Deliverables:

> Report with the assessment result.

> Simplified documentation on the team's product architecture.

> Documentation on testing strategy and technical quality.

WEEK 4: Focus on delivery

Tasks:

> Follow up on deliverables (MVP).

> Conduct analysis of tools and work items used by the team.

> Conduct analysis on communication strategies with stakeholders.

Deliverables:

> Presentation on deliverable status to stakeholders.

> Presentation on the overall progress and learnings.

WEEK 5: Consolidation

Tasks:

> Consolidate the material created during the Sprints (weeks).

> Document pain points, bottlenecks, dependencies, and issues perceived in the engagement, always related to the agile mindset.

Deliverables:

> Summary report of the work done during previous weeks.

> Presentation about pain points, bottlenecks, dependencies, and perceived issues.

WEEK 6: Stakeholder alignment

Tasks:

> Conduct meetings with the main stakeholders (onsite).

> Align on next steps.

Deliverables:

> All materials generated so far, templates and artifacts used by the team.

>> HOW TO UNDERSTAND THE TIMELINE

The previous chapter presented the plan for the six weeks of an Agile consultant's work. The way this work was organized influenced the structure of the book and the way we are going to tell you this story: Sprint by Sprint, following a chronological order. But before you continue reading, please take some time to understand the timeline.

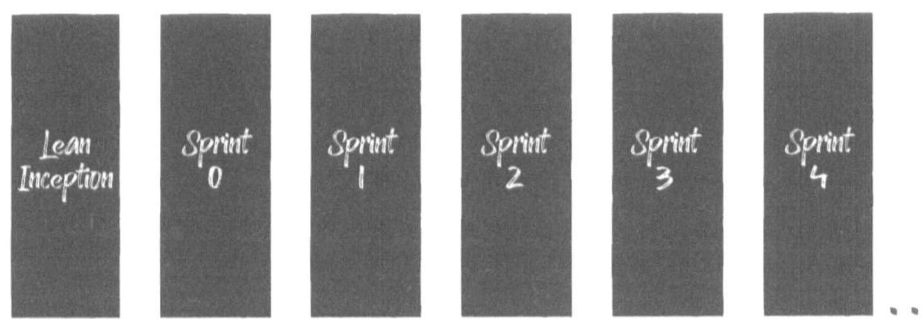

sprints timeline

Lean Inception – Week 1

In the first week, the team attended a Lean Inception workshop. As a result, the team aligned on the schedule and deliverables for the following weeks.

Sprint Zero – Week 2

For teams that use the framework Scrum, the term "Sprint Zero" is common. Although we don't start counting from zero (but from 1), Scrum teams generally refer to the first Sprint as "zero", this being the Sprint dedicated to set-up activities, which do not directly address tasks related to building new product features.

Regardless of using Scrum or another method or framework for managing and monitoring the creation of the product, we suggest using this concept of dedicating some initial time to carry out the initial preparatory tasks. After that, the Sprints should focus on delivering product features.

One-Week Sprints – Weeks 3, 4, 5 and 6

This team used the framework Scrum and worked on 1-week Sprints. So, in the context of this book, please consider that one Sprint equals one week. To avoid confusion about the weeks number versus Sprints number, please follow the following list that maps weeks and Sprints according to how the team referred to them:

- » **Week 1:** Lean Inception.
- » **Week 2:** Sprint 0.
- » **Week 3:** Sprint 1.
- » **Week 4:** Sprint 2.
- » **Week 5:** Sprint 3.
- » **Week 6:** Sprint 4 (At this time, Caroli, who was the Agile consultant, stopped working with the team, but kept in touch with Mary and they continued writing this book).
- » And so it continued until Sprint 20, when Mary stopped working with the team.

Weeks and days

We've structured the following parts by weeks and, within them, by chapters representing the days (for example: Week 2 / Day 8 – Notes from a Daily Scrum). The book started on the 1st, which was a Monday. Day 6 and 7 were, respectively, Saturday and Sunday and week 2 started on the 8th. It should be noted that the team never worked on weekends.

WEEK 1

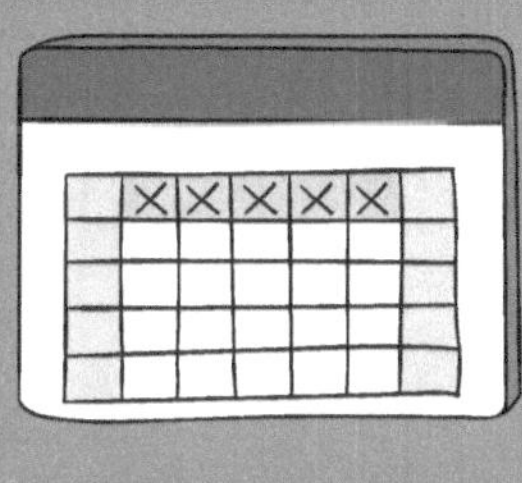

WEEK 1

≫ *DAY 1 TO 5* **LEAN INCEPTION**

Lean Inception is the name given to the collaborative workshop designed to align a group of people on the minimum viable product to be built. It uses Design Thinking[26] techniques with a Lean Startup approach.[27]

Before starting to build the product, the team participates in a collaborative workshop with a sequence of activities to align and define objectives, strategies, and the product scope.

Lean Inception agenda

Here's the team schedule for the Lean Inception week:

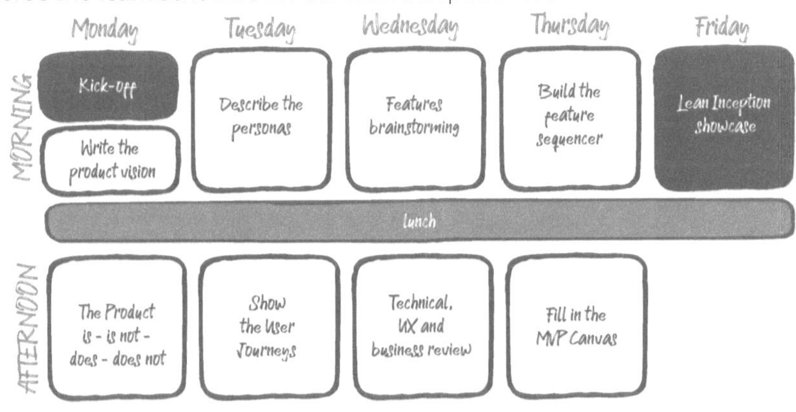

---

26 Brown, Tim. *Change by Design: How Design Thinking Transforms Organizations and Inspires Innovation.* USA: Harper Business, 2009.

27 Ries, Eric. *The Lean Startup: How Today's Entrepreneurs Use Continuous Innovation to Create Radically Successful Businesses.* USA: Currency, 2011.

To learn more about all the steps of this collaborative workshop, we recommend reading the book *Lean Inception*.

Outcome of the workshop

The main results achieved in the Lean Inception workshop were:

> » Improvements on several areas (knowledge, relationship, and commitment of everyone involved).
>
> » Product backlog and Minimum Viable Product (MVP) strategy.
>
> » Shared understanding of the MVP and product increments.

Knowledge, relationship, and commitment

These are the three main benefits that come from a *Lean Inception*. Those who participate in the Lean Inception week acquire a high level of knowledge about the product to be built. They also build a connection and a good relationship with the others involved in the process of building the product, in addition to assuming a high level of commitment with the dates and deliverables agreed upon during the Lean Inception.

However, imagine someone who did not participate in the Lean Inception workshop and, after some time – days or weeks – joins the team that is working on building the product's MVP. This new team member does not have the same level of knowledge, relationship, and commitment as the participants of the Lean Inception. It is very important to emphasize this aspect. As much as this new member quickly understands the details of the MVP to be built, they will need help and time to consolidate knowledge, relationship, and commitment to match what the team has already established.

Product release plan via MVP and increments

The image below demonstrates the feature sequencer, a tangible result of the Lean Inception: the product release plan via MVP.

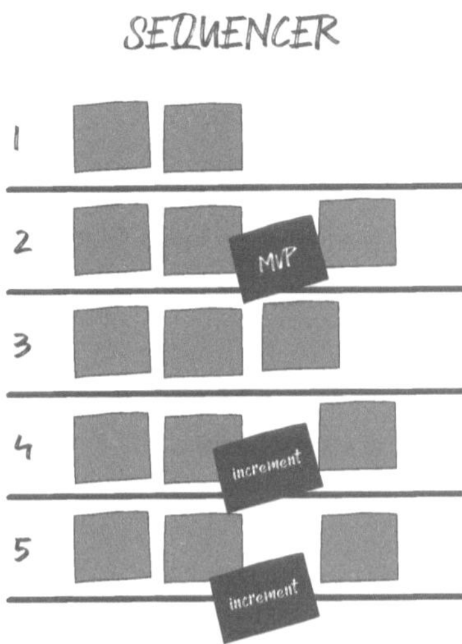

Minimum Viable Product (MVP)

MVP is the simplest version of a product that can be made available. It determines which features are most essential to have a first increment of a product that can add value to the business (minimum product) and that can be effectively used and validated by the end user (viable product).

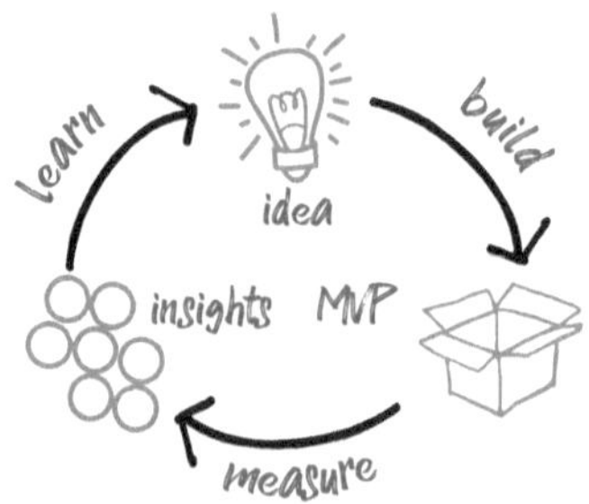

In the initial phases of more traditional projects (agile or waterfall), the focus was on generating the product release plan, often quite comprehensive. In the Lean Inception, the focus is on the MVP, the minimum viable product. We think about the final result, but we only align on and plan the MVP.

In more traditional projects we planned and created a lot of features that weren't used (and with that, a lot of time and money was wasted). In the Lean Inception, we decide on only the MVP and the first product increments. Then, with feedback from users and the business, we determine the next steps. The "Minimum Viable Product" chapter at the beginning of this book will give you more details on this concept.

One of the main artifacts created in the Lean Inception is the MVP Canvas, which displays the details of the MVP. The following is an example of an MVP Canvas:

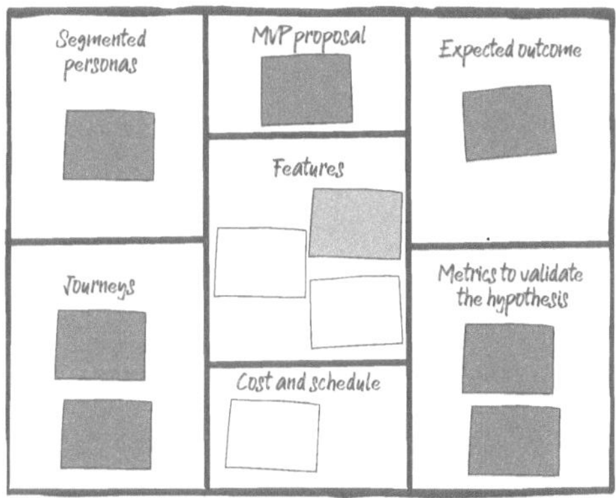

Team learning

After spending five days working together in a room, we learned important lessons that could take weeks, or even months, to identify. In addition to the main outcomes already mentioned, the important lessons learned by this team during Lean Inception were:

» The client believed they were sure of the product backlog and had all the details well defined. By bringing in people from outside the client's context, we raised questions for which we didn't have the answers at the time, and with that, we were able to organize ourselves to iteratively reduce uncertainty and risk.

» Initially, our Product Owner believed that it would not be necessary to be present in the day-to-day of the development team and that some developers could be partially allocated. After talking about the product and how we would work together, it was possible to align expectations regarding the presence of the PO in the team's routine and the dedication of the developers.

» When conducting Lean Inception in the client's environment, we had several interruptions and absences where people had to participate in other meetings. The big lesson learned here is to prioritize a neutral place where people won't be interrupted.

WEEK 2

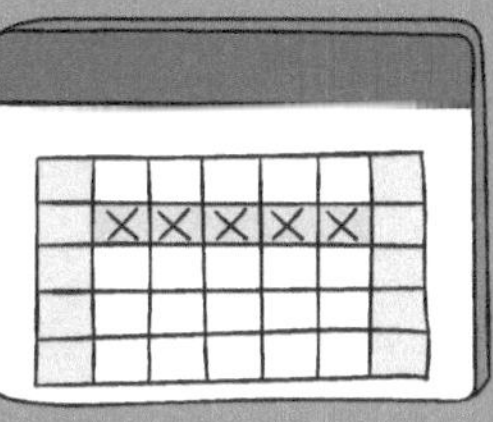

WEEK 2

>> DAY 8 NOTES OF A DAILY SCRUM

Here are some notes taken during a Daily Scrum.

TDD[28]

"So-and-so is teaching me about TDD. You've already gained a loyal follower."
This is a simple comment that demonstrates some really cool aspects:

- » The team preaches for technical excellence, hence the interest in TDD.
- » One person knows more about the business, another about automated testing; both are pairing up, both learning and developing as they work.
- » People on the team have known each other for a few days, but already communicate in a friendly way.

Top-to-bottom Daily Scrum style

The team is reading and updating each task in progress, from top to bottom. Later that day, the team was emailed about the Daily Scrum styles.[29]

Following the order of cards in Trello, the team answers the following questions:

- » What did we do on this task yesterday?

---

28 In the chapter "Technical and theoretical content", in the first section of this book, there is an explanatory part on this subject.

29 Idem.

>> What are we going to do on this task today?

>> What, if anything, is blocking progress on this task?

Where is the UX designer?

""Is the UX guy around today?" asked the developer.

"He is involved in several projects, I will try to locate him," replied the PO

This conversation demonstrates that the team does not have a dedicated UX person. User experience is essential. The best scenario would be to have this person who represents the end users available to the team at all times. By the way, that person must be part of the team (as in the Spotify model: this person belongs to this product's squad and to the UX chapter).

However, as this person is shared across multiple teams, they should be available in the Daily Scrum and in planning and review meetings. The risk is that the team will keep working, regardless of the UX designer. This can lead to two bad situations:

1. the work does not consider user experience (UX); or

2. there will be rework when the UX designer senses misdirection.

Tech huddle

"I finished test case X; we have to decide if this is unit testing or UI testing," said one developer.

And that led the Daily Scrum to get into a good conversation about testing, where they should be, what naming convention to use, what structure, etc. But the conversation became very technical and would be a good candidate for a tech huddle, a more technical meeting to talk about a specific subject.

RETROSPECTIVE INVITATION

Below is the invitation sent to the team:

Team,

Let's use this remote board for our retrospective: <link>.

Please bring your laptop as we will be using one for each participant in this remote meeting.

Here is the meeting agenda:

1. **Context**: Let's talk about how we will interact with each other in our day to day work. Collectively, we will define the team's agreements.

2. **Prime directive for team building**: "Cooperation is the act of working with others and acting together to accomplish a job. Team is a partnership of unique people who bring out the very best in each other, and who know that even though they are wonderful as individuals, they are even better together. Coming together is a beginning; keeping together is progress; working together is success."

3. **Energizer**: Surprise.

4. **Check-in:** One Word.

5. **Main course:** Defining the team's agreements (we'll use the FunRetrospectives link).

6. **Filtering:** Dot voting.

7. **Checkout:** What-who-when.

   Cheers.

   Caroli and Mary pairing up.

DEFINING THE TEAM AGREEMENTS

As this was the team's first retrospective, we used the meeting to set work agreements. A team building activity was carried out with the purpose of defining the team agreements.

It follows the meeting agenda, in seven steps, according to the blog post *A 7-Step Agenda for Effective Retrospectives.*[30]

1. Context

Talk about how we will interact with each other in our daily work. Collectively, we will define our team's agreements for each of these areas:

- » Purpose and agenda of meetings.
- » Preferred method of communication.
- » Responsibilities and availability.
- » Processes and ways of working.

2. Prime directive

We read the team building prime directive:

---

30 Caroli, Paulo. *A 7 step agenda for effective retrospectives.* Available at: www.caroli. org/a-7-step- agendafor-effective-retrospectives/. Accessed on: March 2020.

> Cooperation is the act of working with others and acting together to accomplish a job. Team is a partnership of unique people who bring out the very best in each other, and who know that even though they are wonderful as individuals, they are even better together. Coming together is a beginning; keeping together is progress; working together is success.

3. Energizer

We did the energizing activity *Ping Pong*. The activity was more difficult given the presence of remote participants, which is an excellent point of reflection on the communication difficulties found in remote teams.

4. Check-in

Each participant spoke a word about how they were feeling at that time, given the context of the meeting. The activity used was *One Word*.

5. Main Course

We used the *Defining the Team Agreements* activity to help the team collectively define and write the agreements. We used *FunRetrospectives* as a tool for remote collaboration.

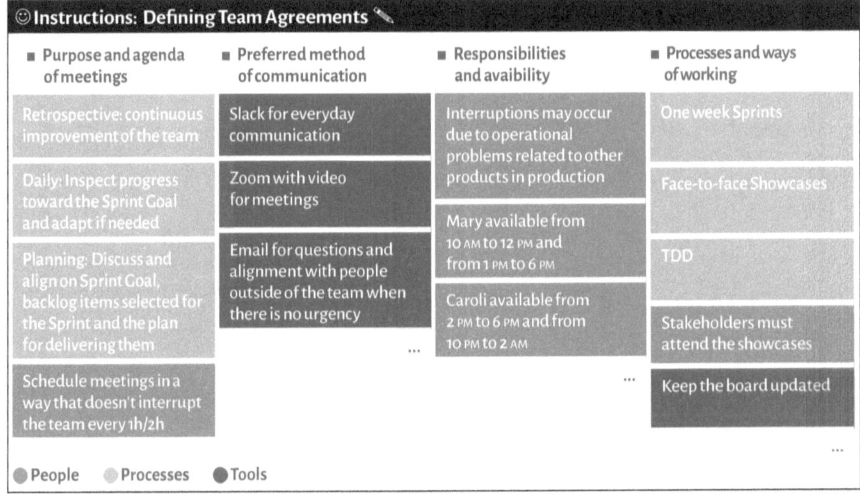

6. Filtering

Each participant had six votes. The cards were sorted by the most voted, and then we talked about them.

7. Checkout

An email with action items (*What-Who-When*) and retrospective notes was sent to all participants.

EMAIL WITH
RETROSPECTIVE NOTES

Team,

Below are some notes captured during our meeting. The link to our remote board in *FunRetrospectives* is still available for anyone who wants to check all the cards.

Meetings:

› One week Sprints.

› Thirty-minute Sprint Planning: everyone must read the cards and write in the description.

› Sprint Planning on Mondays, from 11 am to 11:30 am.

› Sprint Review on Fridays, from 4 pm to 4:30 pm.

› Retrospective every two weeks: on Fridays from 4:30 pm to 5:30 pm.

› Daily Scrum every day at 11 am.

› Showcase on MVP delivery and major product increments (to schedule with stakeholders).

Communication:

› Everyday communication on Slack.

› Meetings via Zoom.

› React on Slack with thumbs-up to show that you've read the message.

› Email frequency: use email only when there's no urgency, many on the team only access email once a day.

› Keep a communication channel open: Zoom meeting open all day on the TV with audio on and microphone muted. When someone wants to talk, they must unmute and talk to the rest of the team in the other location.

› Keep the board up to date.

Cheers,

Caroli and Mary pairing up.

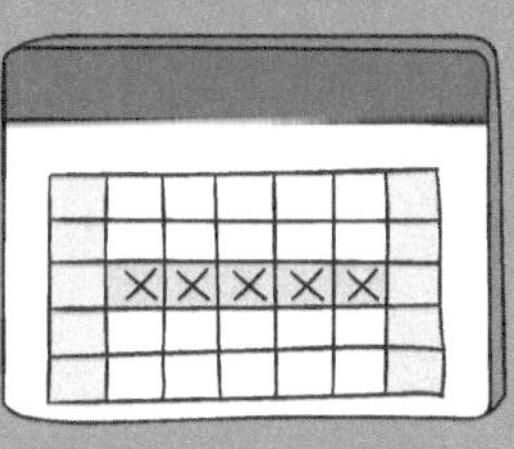

WEEK 3

❯❯ DAY 15 THE SPRINT MEETINGS

The team worked on each item of the team agreements. During the meeting, it was clear that the team uses the Scrum framework (to learn more, see the chapter "An Overview of Scrum" at the beginning of this book).

Below is the schedule of the Sprint meetings agreed upon by the team. These meetings were scheduled by Mary, who played the role of the team's Scrum Master. This drawing was posted on the wall and was visible to everyone on the team.

* Although the team decided to do retrospectives every two weeks, in the first few Sprints the team tried to maintain the weekly team building activities as they were starting to work together.

Day 15 – Challenges in the Sprint Planning

The Sprint started with a planning meeting that wasn't very effective: the meeting was long and the backlog on the team's board wasn't quite refined."[31]

Given the problem, we wrote the following email to the team:

Team,

Looking at our board we can see that the stories/tasks are not well defined to be planned. This is relatively normal in early planning meetings.

To improve this, we have two suggestions: 1. Create a checklist so that a story/task is considered ready to be included in the planning; and 2. Schedule a refinement meeting (formerly called grooming), which must precede the Sprint Planning.

For 2, we suggest maintaining the efficiency of the planning and review meetings: 30-minute meetings. We will work on item 1.

Cheers,

Caroli and Mary pairing up.

One day after this email, we worked on item 1, and the result was the "Definition of Ready Checklist".

---

31 The original term which gave the name to a Scrum ceremony: grooming. But the word has another meaning, which is why the Scrum people changed the name of the meeting from grooming to refinement.

>> DAY 16 DEFINITION OF READY CHECKLIST

Team,

Attached is the checklist that Mary and I created as a suggestion.

We are going to use it in the backlog refinement session we have

tomorrow at 11:30 am.

Cheers,

Caroli.

Definition of Ready Checklist

Each work item (User Story, task, etc.) candidate for a Sprint Planning must pass this checklist. A negative answer indicates that the item is not ready to go into planning.

☑ *Item ready for the Sprint Planning:*

Do I have the information I need to do the work?
☐ No
☐ Yes, please specify:

Do I know why we need this work item?
☐ No
☐ Yes, please specify:

Do I know how to show the completion of this work item?
☐ No
☐ Yes, please specify:

Can I relate this work item to an epic or expected outcome?
☐ No
☐ Yes, please specify:

Does this work item fit in a Sprint?
☐ No, item must be broken into smaller units
☐ Yes

Context: Why was the checklist created?

After the Sprint Planning the day before, it was possible to see that this meeting would not be as productive as it could have been. The team kept turning over questions that could not be answered in that conversation. Or, because it was the first time they were looking at a work item, they didn't know how to answer key questions about it. This made it difficult to break the work down into smaller items or even prioritize them in order to reduce dependencies and deliver value sooner.

Another factor that contributed to the creation of the checklist was the PO's availability. As the PO was also working with other teams and initiatives, he didn't have time to get all the information needed to provide clarity and context to the team before the Sprint Planning.

In this context, creating a checklist made a lot of sense, as it served as support for the team to prepare and ensure that all items at the top of the backlog had all the necessary details so as not to put the Sprint at risk. In this way, it became possible to establish and commit to the Sprint goal.

>> DAY 16 DEVOPS ASSESSMENT

After two weeks, we decided to apply the DevOps assessment,[32] on the code that the team received. The plan was to do it again in four weeks' time to check for improvements and decide on the next steps.

Below is the result and the reasoning behind each grade.

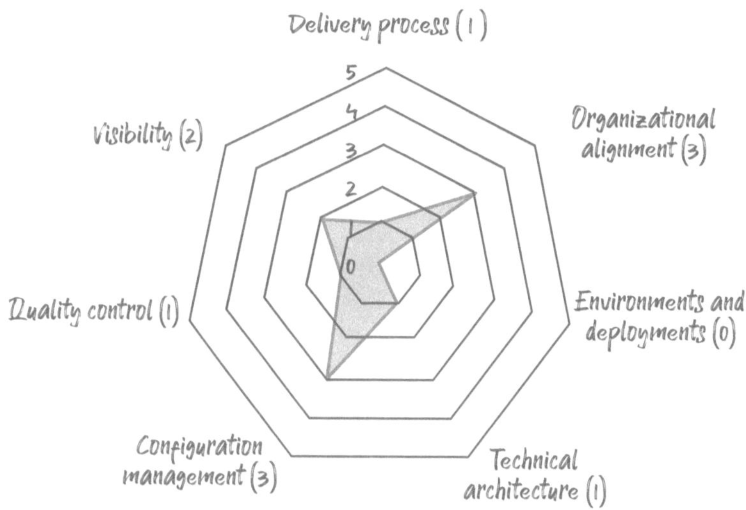

DevOps assessement result – Legacy

---

32 In the first section of this book, there is an explanatory chapter on this subject. You can download this assessment at: https://caroli.org/en/continuous-delivery-assessment/.

Delivery process

Grade: 1

> There was a pattern of branches (gitflow style) and there was a manual test, when an "OK" came back, the artifacts were sent by email.

Quality control

Grade: 1

> Android project didn't have any kind of tests; iOS had a few unit tests.

> Manual tests (table tests) were performed at each product release.

> It's the support team that tracks bugs.

Configuration management

Grade: 3

> Both Android and iOS already used the dependency manager – Gradle and Cocoapots. They already used Git.

Environments and deployments

Grade: 0

> We don't have a complete test environment (there is a QA01 for the back-end, but no mobile test environment).

> We don't have CI. Every deployment process is manual (with APK back and forth via email).

Data storage

Grade: not applicable

> Our product is just middleware, no database.

Technical architecture

Grade: 1

> The code is highly coupled. We don't have anything automated. It is very difficult to unit test the code. But version-based dependency management already exists.

Organizational alignment

Grade: 3

> There is an open channel of communication with the product teams (which consume our SDK).

> There is a bit of knowledge separation, for example one person knows Android, the other knows iOS.

Visibility

Grade: 2

> We have the release history in Git.

> The team started using Trello to give visibility to their tasks.

>> DAY 17 DAILY SCRUM PARKING LOT SUGGESTION

Below is the email in which the adoption of the Parking Lot in the Daily Scrum was suggested.

Team,

Congratulations on the Daily Scrum. Punctual, informative and with everyone present. We are following the Daily Scrum Top Down style.[33] A recommendation: when we go into the more technical details about a task/story (today's example: unit, UI, or integration tests. How to decide?), consider putting it in the Parking Lot[34] (or even discuss it in a tech huddle) at the end of the Daily Scrum. That way, those who don't want to participate in the specific conversation can leave after the end of the meeting.

If everyone on the team participates in every conversation, we're going to complain that we don't have time to work.

Cheers, Caroli and Mary pairing up.

---

33 In the chapter "Technical and theoretical content", in the first section of this book, there is an explanatory part on this subject.

34 This technique helps to momentarily park any items, ideas or issues that are raised during a meeting or workshop but are not useful for discussion at that particular time. It is an essential tool for the facilitator as it provides a polite way of saying 'yes, I heard you' and this conversation will be resumed later".

>> DAY 18 RETROSPECTIVE AGENDA FOR SPRINT 1

The following is the email sent with the agenda for the first Sprint retrospective:

Team,

Here's the agenda for our retrospective tomorrow.

1. **Context:** We are in the first step, creating the path to production. We are using weeklong Sprints. Let's look at this last Sprint and talk about what went right and what we can improve on.

2. **Prime directive for retrospectives:** "Regardless of what we discover, we understand and truly believe that everyone did the best job they could, given what they knew at the time, their skills and abilities, the resources available, and the situation at hand".

3. **Energizer:** Let's repeat the *Ping Pong* activity. In the last retrospective, we had difficulty dealing with this activity, especially because of the remote factor. Let's see if we improve this time.

4. **Check-in:** Let's use the *Safety Check* activity in *FunRetrospectives*.

5. **Main course:** Let's use the *Small Starfish* activity in *FunRetrospectives*.

6. **Filtering:** Each participant will have five votes. The cards will be sorted by the most voted and we'll talk about them.

7. **Checkout:** We talk at the end of the meeting.

   Cheers,

   Caroli and Mary pairing up.

» DAY 19 RETROSPECTIVE

The retrospective started as planned. The check-in activity used was the *Safety Check*. Below is the result:

FunRetrospectives	
	Safety Check
	Choose the one that best indicates how safe you feel:
Votes	
2	No problem, I'll talk about anything.
5	I'll talk about almost everything; some subjects may be more difficult.
3	I'll talk about some things, but others will be difficult to say.
0	I won't say much; I'll let others raise the issues.
0	I will smile, say everything is fine, and agree with the managers.

Given the check-in result, it made no sense to follow the planned agenda for the retrospective, in which the main activity would be the *Small Starfish*. We could not continue with a planned context of talking about technical improvements, as some people in the team did not feel safe to speak.

So we decided to change the retrospective agenda: we switched the remote board of *Small Starfish* to a board of "Creating Safety."

Here's the new agenda for the retrospective after the check-in activity:

» Main course: *Creating Safety*.

» *Filtering*: Each participant cast five votes on the items in the ideas column to overcome possible causes of lack of safety.

» *Checkout*: We read and talked about the items raised and finally everyone voted again on a new *Safety Check* board.

Below is an example of a *Creating Safety* board.

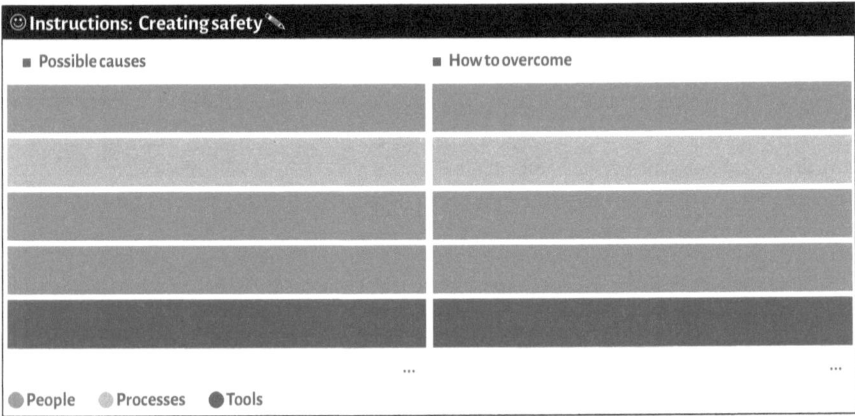

See also how the new *Safety Check* board, carried out at the end of the retrospective, looked like after the conversation about "Creating Safety".

FunRetrospectives	
	Safety Check
	Choose the one that best indicates how safe you feel:
Votes	
5	No problem, I'll talk about anything.
3	I'll talk about almost everything; some subjects may be more difficult.
2	I'll talk about some things, but others will be difficult to say.
0	I won't say much; I'll let others raise the issues.
0	I will smile, say everything is fine, and agree with the managers.

Reflecting on this retrospective

The retrospective check-in activity was essential. It clearly demonstrated that the team needed to talk not only about how to work, but also about how to feel safer in order to share ideas and opinions.

This is a very common event in teams' formation: starting to work and prioritizing conversations about work before getting to know each other as a team.

Therefore, team building activities are essential, especially when people are starting to work together.

» DAY 19 RETROSPECTIVE ACTION ITEMS' EMAIL

Below is the email sent with the action items from the Sprint 1 Retrospective:

Team,

Thank you very much for participating in the retrospective. You raised very important points for excellent teamwork.

This retrospective style doesn't generate a lot of action items, but rather an awareness and respect for what's important to each and every person on the team.

As action items, I only have these two:

Check the best day for the planning meeting; Mondays do not work for the UX designer: let's raise this when we go through the Parking Lot at the end of the next Daily Scrum.

Schedule short sessions for people to introduce themselves and get to know each other: I'm going to use an activity for that purpose in our next retrospective.

Cheers,

Caroli.

WEEK 4

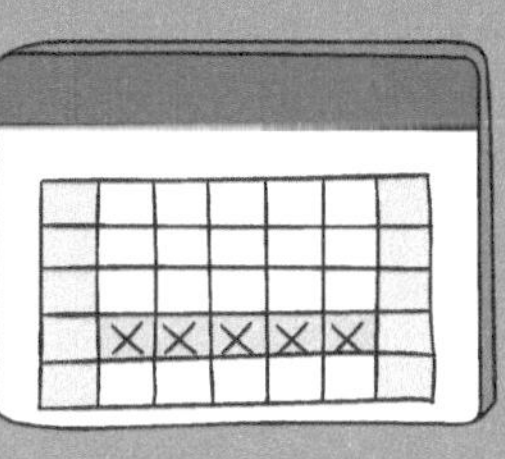

SPRINT PLANNING

During the Sprint Planning meeting, the team discussed the current state of work, upcoming work items, and commitment to the Sprint that was starting. They also debated about effort, time, and the Sprint goal. In addition, the team checked the features sequencer (output of the Lean Inception) to remind them of the commitment to the MVP expected date.

A work item was rewritten. It was "a little big to get into the Sprint" (the item fell into the fine mesh of the Definition of Ready Checklist). The item was rewritten as two separate items, each one went through the checklist, and then were added to the Sprint backlog.

≫ DAY 23 "WHAT" VERSUS "HOW" EMAIL

Team,

Earlier today I attended the payments flow discussion meeting, and I realized something that I think is important to share, especially for everyone's participation in future Lean Inceptions.

During Lean Inception week, I would sometimes remind the team that at that time we were interested in understanding what we should be doing. And I told the group that after the Lean Inception, during the Sprints, when the time came, we would detail how we were going to do it.

Remember that advertisement: "I am you tomorrow"? Whoever remembers is revealing their age!

Today was an example of a session detailing the how. We did get into detail of three User Stories. Well done!

Cheers,

Caroli.

» DAY 24 *THE USER STORIES OF THE FIRST FEATURES*

Team,

Do you remember the features sequencer from the Lean Inception?

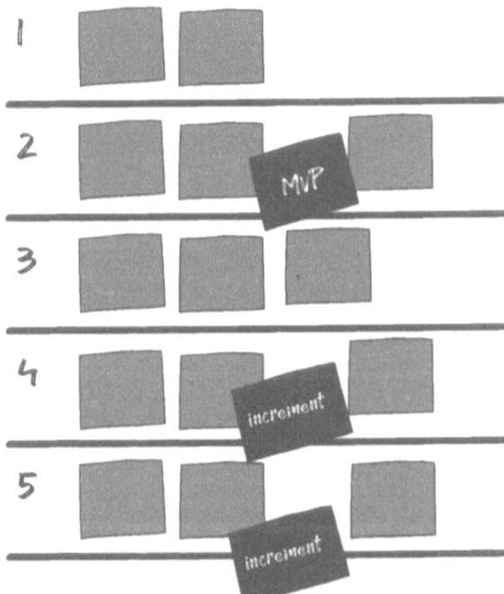

So, following our planning, this week we started with the features in the first line of the sequencer.

We are still finishing some tasks from the first iteration, from path to production, the non-functional tasks, the work of

improvement/adaptation/creation of the infrastructure needed to start with the functional code.

Looking at our board, the current plan for user stories and initial tasks, and listening to the conversations about the Continuous Delivery pipeline, we seem to be doing well, that means: We had sucess in setting the stage to start working on the MVP features.

Now we need to refine the following work items:

› Review error messages (Android).

› Review error messages (iOS).

Let's use the Definition of Ready Checklist to help us verify that the work item (User Story or task, as you prefer) is ready for the Sprint Planning meeting.

Next week we will have a slightly different agenda. We'll have the refinement meeting on Monday and the planning meeting on Tuesday.

However, if you already want to anticipate this work, please contact us.

Cheers,

Caroli and Mary pairing up.

DAY 26 TEAM BUILDING ACTIVITY

Below is the email with the agenda for the team building activity, which aims to make the team to get to know each other better.

Team,

This is the agenda of the team building activity, an action item from our last retrospective. We'll start in five minutes.

1. **Context:** We want to get to know each other better.

2. **Prime directive for team building:** "Cooperation is the act of working with others and acting together to accomplish a job. Team is a partnership of unique people who bring out the very best in each other, and who know that even though they are wonderful as individuals, they are even better together. Coming together is a beginning; keeping together is progress; working together is success."

3. **Main course:** Let's use *The Roles We Play* activity, by accessing the board link in *FunRetrospectives*.

Cheers,

Caroli and Mary pairing up.

In this activity, each person wrote their various roles (before, during, after work and on weekends) on the board. Then we read all the cards one by one.

Below is the reproduction of the *FunRetrospectives* board at the end of the activity.

☺ **Instructions:** ✏

■ Before work	■ At work	■ After work	■ Weekend
[VT] Dad	[FD] Developer	[LR] Video game player	[JB] Barbecue chef
[ER] Mage	[JB] Product Owner	[YN] TV Shows binge watcher / couch potato	[CF] Drunk
[ER] Husband	[VA] Developer	[MP] Bookworm	[ER] Husband
[FD] Dad	[MP] Scrum Master	[JB] Dad	[FD] Student
[JB] Driver	[YN] Developer	...	[MP] Cinephile
...	[VT] Developer		[VT] Father and husband
	[ER] Developer		...
	[CF] UX Designer		
	[GF] Developer		
	[PC] Agile Consultant		
	[LR] Developer		
	...		

WEEK 5

WEEK 5

>> *DAY 29* **IMPROVEMENT FOR BACKLOG REFINEMENT: FEATURES AND STORIES**

The email sent after the backlog refinement meeting follows:

Team,

We had our backlog refinement meeting today, but the user stories we would like to discuss tomorrow in the Sprint Planning, still need some refinement. And we wouldn't write this email without offering help!

Please see the file on Features and User Stories[35] attached to this email. Let's just use one of the three work items in the next step, as an example:

Work item: Review error messages (Android).

Stories (or better, candidates for stories):

> As an Android user, I want to read the error message (with URL) and click on the "Ok" button to close the window — *please confirm the behavior of the button.*

> As an Android user, I want to read the error message (with

---

35 In the first section of this book, there is an explanatory chapter on this subject.

URL) and click on "Contact Us" which leads to the correct channel (the URL) — *how many scenarios are there?*

› As an Android user, I want to read the error message without a line break in the title/label (there is currently a break in the title).

› As an Android user, I want to read the error message with the default colors and fonts of our app — *verify with UX Designer.*

We marked with a * the issues that must be resolved by our UX Designer.

Cheers,

Caroli and Mary pairing up.

 THE ROLE OF PRODUCT OWNER AND TEAM CAPACITY

Below is a draft of an unsent email. The topic could be sensitive, and we decided to have a conversation in person rather than sending the email.

Team,

We have a problem. But I'm not going to talk about the solution in this email, just the problem and adjustments to dates and deliverables.

When we discussed and commited to dates during the Lean Inception, we considered that the developers would be mainly focused on development tasks.

We assumed that both the strategic direction of the product and the detailing of the features in User Stories would be a job primarily carried out by the Product Owner (I'm not talking about who is nominally the PO of this team, but the PO role itself, this is a long conversation and it is not only about this team).

Today, after the backlog refinement meeting, I stopped to reflect and realized that the decisions about the product and its details are primarily being carried out by the developers. An example of this is creating spikes to make product decisions.

Given that this is our scenario, we need to revise the dates according to the team's capacity.

My suggestion: redo the team capacity calculation and re-validate expected dates for the product increments.

Cheers,

Caroli.

>> DAY 30 BACKLOG REFINEMENT

Some team members met to refine the stories and to prepare them for the next Sprint Planning.

The way we called this meeting varied from Backlog refinement meeting to pre-planning meeting. Regardless of the name, it aimed to break down features into stories. Another important point is that the participation of everyone on the Scrum team was not mandatory (unlike the Sprint Planning which only took place with everyone present: UX Designer, developers, Product Owner and Scrum Master).

The following is a representation of the meeting in which the team is refining a work item into a User Story, represented as a card in Trello. This story, along with other well-written User Stories would be part of the next Sprint Backlog.

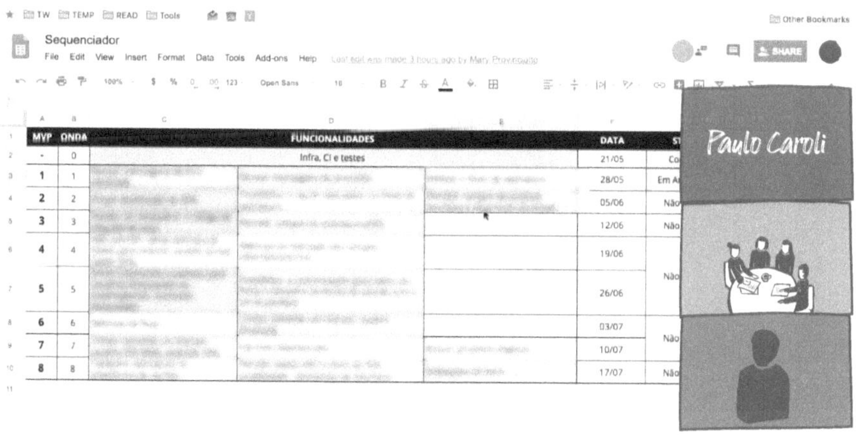

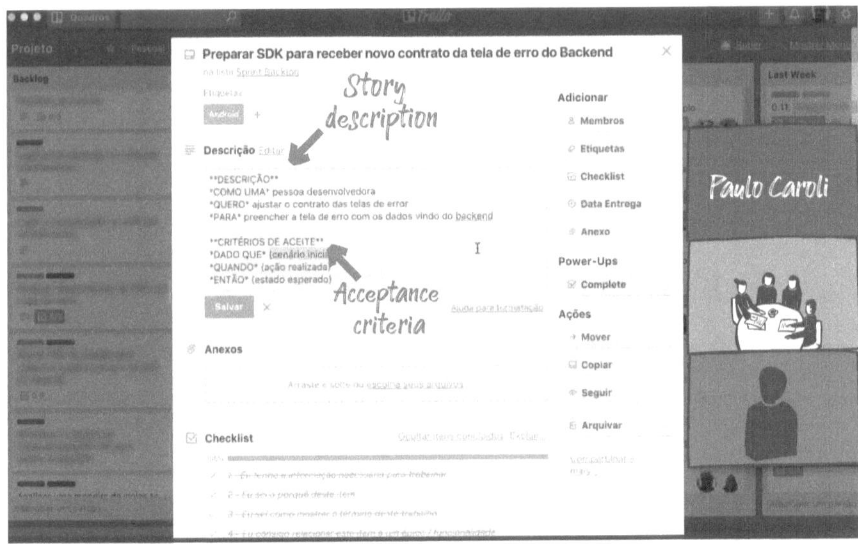

In the image below, observe the team talking about the details — screen by screen — of the mobile app's flow. This generated a lot of discussions to check stories and especially the acceptance criteria (and test scenarios).

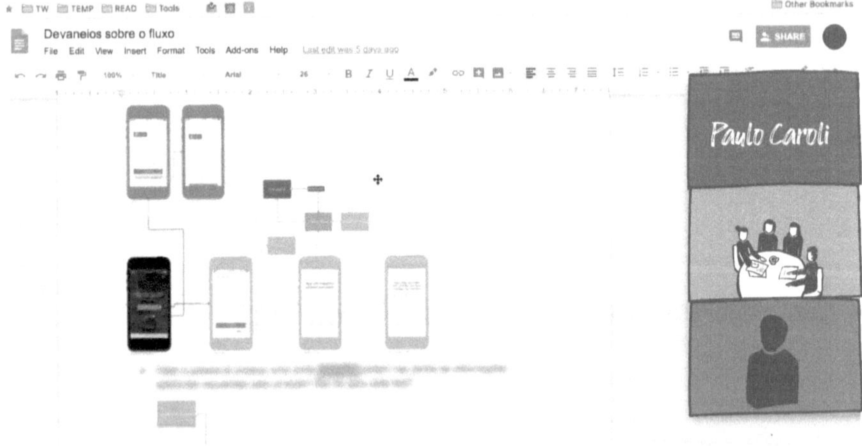

A more detailed conversation is very common during Backlog refinement: technical details, flow, test scenarios, architecture, tasks, etc. This is the time to detail the work to be done. Remembering that, in the next meeting, the Sprint Planning, the team will commit to the work for the next Sprint: the Sprint backlog.

The User Story template in Trello

Each story card on Trello began with the following text that was rewritten by the team:

User Story description

» *As a* ________________________ (role/profile)

» *I want to* ________________________ (action to be performed/product-specific feature)

» *So that* ________________________ (value achieved)

Acceptance criteria

» *Given* ________________________ (initial scenario)

» *When* ________________________ (action performed)

» *Then* ________________________ (expected state)

After writing the description, acceptance criteria, and story details, the team went throught the Definition of Ready Checklist questions.

⊡ **User Story Title**

in list Sprint Backlog

Notifications

◉ Watch

≣ **Description**   Edit

Description
As a <role/profile>
I want to <action/activity>
so that <benefit/reason>

Acceptance Criteria
GIVEN (some scenario)
WHEN (some action is carried out)
THEN (particular set of consequences that should be observed)

☑ **Checklist**   Delete

0%

1 - Do I have the information I need to work?

2- Do I know why we need this work item?

3 - Do I know how to show the completion of this work item?

4 - Can I relate this work item to an epic or expected feature?

⊡ **User Story Title**

in list Sprint Backlog

Notifications

◉ Watch

≣ **Description**   Edit

Description
As a <role/profile>
I want to <action/activity>
so that <benefit/reason>

Acceptance Criteria
GIVEN (some scenario)
WHEN (some action is carried out)
THEN (particular set of consequences that should be observed)

☑ **Checklist**   Hide checked items   Delete

100%

☑ 1 - Do I have the information I need to work?

☑ 2 - Do I know why we need this work item?

☑ 3 - Do I know how to show the completion of this work item?

☑ 4 - Can I relate this work item to an epic or expected feature?

≫ DAY 31 THE PO IS MISSED (VERY MUCH) BY THE TEAM

The PO is missed by the team.
Without the PO the team is like a boat adrift.

This sentence refers to the day a meeting was canceled because the Product Owner was absent. Lean Inception helps with alignment on getting started on the product under construction. The people involved in creating the product (usually called squad or active members) decide the MVP and its features. Everything is beautiful and perfect for starting the work, but that's not enough!

No, it's not just a Lean Inception that will generate a successful product. That's not what we've seen in most places we worked. But before starting to work on the MVP features, the team needs to describe the work in more detail. That's when the real Scrum begins.

Scrum is a term that comes from Rugby. Scrum, an abbreviation of Scrummage, describes the moment when players are head to head, entwined, trying to gain possession of the ball.

That's what happens to teams of innovative companies that are challenged to create transformative digital products. Thinking heads together, all people teamed together to stay in the game.

This interweaving and meshing is essential for successful product creation.

Even though it started with a Lean Inception, with the "North direction" and the MVP plan well defined.

The moment of truth is when we are breaking down MVP features into smaller, more chewy, more testable, more workable chunks; that's when things get difficult (when the pig twists the tail.)[36]

We chose this expression because we remember that joke in which the pig and the chicken talk about opening a restaurant that serves breakfast, called "Eggs with Bacon." The chicken is involved (it provides the eggs), while the pig is commited (its skin — the bacon — is in the game). The point is that the squad, the product team, and each one of those engaged in the day-to-day Sprint meetings represents the pig, and as part of those who are commited, one has an essential role: the PO.

The Product Owner, the person responsible for the strategic direction of the product, is the one who slices, discards, refines and prioritizes the work during the team ceremonies: Daily Scrum, Sprint Planning, Sprint Review, Retrospective, and backlog refinement meetings.

See in this image how Spotify (a widely used example for organizing teams) organizes itself into teams. Note the relationship between the team and the PO: there is no one without the other.

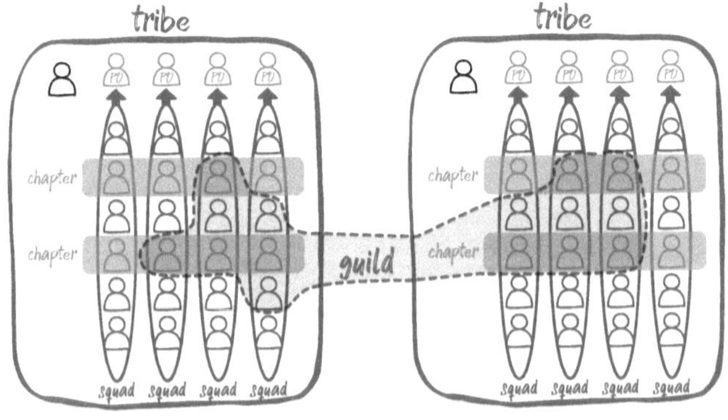

---

36 Popular expression in Brazil used to describe challenging situations

A team without the PO is a boat adrift. It may even get somewhere, but no one guarantees that this is the place it should go.

If your organization is like a small boat, maybe that's not a problem: keep sailing and, from time to time, check where you want to go, aligning the boat's direction.

But this is not the case for large organizations, with several boats of various sizes, with a common destination. Someone, or rather "someones" need to align all these boats in relation to the direction of the company.

Don't think about stopping all the crew to decide the direction and then go back to their boats to sail towards that direction. This only works in small companies, with few boats.

Promote encounters between all POs to align the strategic direction among all teams. This is probably not done just once, but frequently instead. After all, everyone is still sailing, but the waters, winds and weather will change, and it will be necessary to rethink the path and realign plans according to the latest developments.

But don't leave teams without the Product Owner for too long. The PO can attend other meetings, but still remains the ship's captain! If the PO is absent for a long time, the boat may go adrift.

To help with this, Scrum has well-defined meetings, which require the presence of the PO. POs actively participate in Sprint meetings. That's why they are able to guide and help the team to navigate according to the greatest interest: the strategic direction of the organization and all teams.

>> DAY 33 WE NEED A RETROSPECTIVE

Until last week, the team was working on all the tasks of the path to production, creating the continuous delivery pipeline, preparing the environments and tools necessary to create the functional code. This week the team started working on the MVP features.

However, the beginning was troubled:

- » Stories were not well written and understood (inefficient refinement sessions).
- » The planning meeting took more than two hours (the desired duration was half an hour).
- » The team was working on several spikes, as there were changes in the work decisions to be carried out for the first features agreed during the Lean Inception.
- » Last Sprint Retrospective was canceled.

All this happened within a week. Agile teams work with an inspection and adaptation mindset, which is systematically addressed in the retrospective meeting.

As this meeting had been canceled, an email was sent with the aim of rescheduling it and avoiding the cancelation of future retrospectives.

Good morning,

Do you prefer a retrospective today or on Monday? "Every team must do one retrospective per week unless they are too busy. In that case you must do two!".

I always repeat that phrase. And I try to do a retrospective a week on all the teams I work. I've never regretted doing this often, but I regretted the opposite: not doing retrospectives very often. For a team like ours, with a complex context and small increments, MVP style, one retrospective per week is highly recommended.

Last week we canceled a retrospective, and it seems to me that we have the feeling that we are out of time given the existence of so many (inefficient) meetings and work to do. This gives me the signal that we need to prioritize the conversation about how to improve the way we work: we need a retrospective.

Cheers,

Caroli.

After everyone responded to the email, we scheduled the retrospective for Monday.

Direct communication

The email sent has a direct question: Would you rather do a retrospective today or on Monday?

Note that this email only gives you two response options: today or Monday.

It is important to note that people receive a lot of emails, they will probably read this message in ten seconds and will need to jump to the next task. So, simplify their lives by being direct and intentional.

Don't start an email dialogue with, "Hi, the retrospective is very important, do you agree?" or "Can we reschedule the retrospective meeting? What day is best for you?"

Go straight to the point. If you have a CTA (Call To Action), be objective and intentional. This email and its result exemplifies this!

>> DAY 33 CONVERSATION WITH DEVELOPERS

We had the feeling that the motivation of the developers had dropped. And we needed a way to visualize the issue and bring that insight to the PO and stakeholders: a retrospective.

Not a retrospective for the whole team, but just for the developers. The context: a chat about how you are feeling as part of this team, in relation to your work.

Before sharing the activity and the result generated, it is important to emphasize that this does not, in any way, replace the team's retrospective. This was just an "extra" activity to validate and generate input for other conversations.

The activity used was Peaks and Valleys Timeline[37] which uses a simple visual language to share the individual views of each person in the timeline before Lean Inception, during it and in the following steps. Below is the result of the activity.

---

37 The Peaks and Valleys Timeline. FunRetrospectives. Available at: https://www.funretrospectives.com/roles-and-responsibilities/. Accessed on: March, 2023.

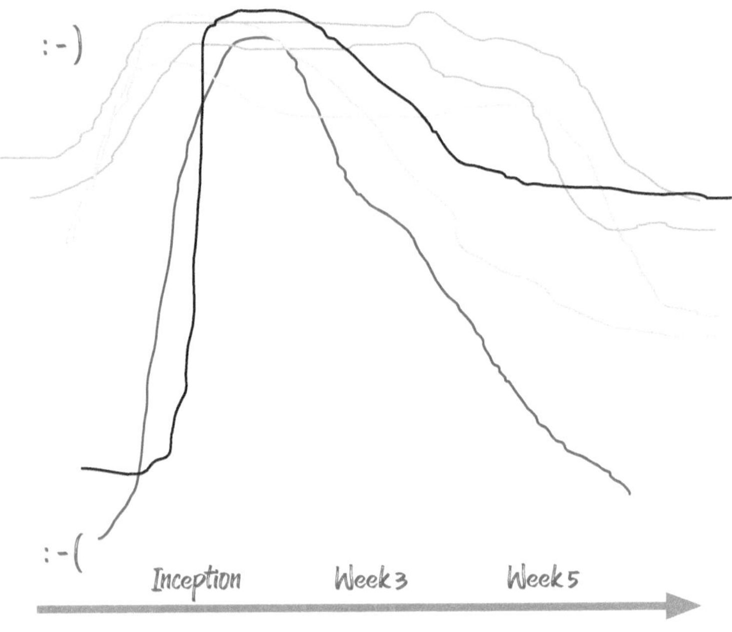

Result of the activity Peaks and Valleys

The image is a representation of the activity performed on Google Drawing, the tool used to carry out the activity remotely.

Each line represents how a person felt over time. It became easier to demonstrate that the developers liked the Lean Inception week, they were "ok" with the first weeks, but that motivation had been dropping since the functional work started in the following weeks.

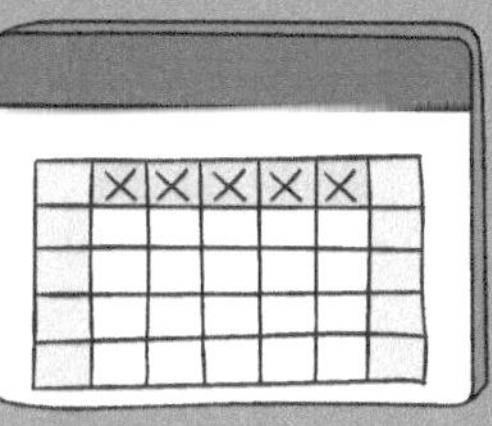

WEEK 6

Team,

Here's the agenda of our retrospective today, which will take place right after our Daily standup, probably from 11:30 am to 12:30 pm.

1. **Context:** We are starting the fourth Sprint. Let's talk about our deliverables – the MVP – and how we're working.

2. **Prime directive for restrospectives:** "Regardless of what we discover, we understand and truly believe that everyone did the best job they could, given what they knew at the time, their skills and abilities, the resources available, and the situation at hand".

3. **Energizer:** Surprise.

4. **Check-in:** *One Word.*

5. **Main course:** *Small Starfish.*

6. **Filtering:** Dot voting (5 votes per participant).

7. **Checkout:** Let's reread the action items, and write a word before leaving: *One Word Before Leaving* activity.

>> DAY 36 RETROSPECTIVE

More details about the execution and also images of the retrospective meeting follow.

Check-in – One Word

See the result of the "One Word" check-in activity in the image. Each person spoke and wrote a word that reflects how they felt at that moment (beginning of the meeting) about the context presented.

FunRetrospectives

One Word
serene
confident
good
motivated
confused
calm
calm
confused
anxious

Main Course – Small Starfish

As the main course, the team was asked to write cards for the three areas of the respective *FunRetrospectives* remote board:

- » *Continue (keep doing):* something the team is doing well and recognizes its value.
- » *More (more of):* something the team is doing and believes it will bring more value if done more often.
- » *Less/Stop:* something the team is doing and has some value, but it is preferable to reduce it little by little or all at once.

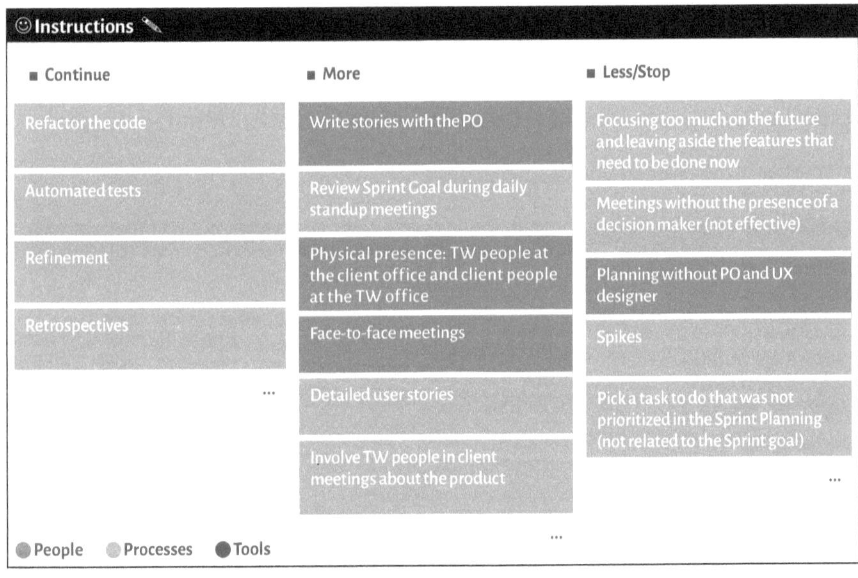

Top rated items during the Small Starfish activity

Filtering – Dot voting

Cards were sorted by number of votes. After the time to write the Small Starfish cards, we re-read and grouped all the cards together without talking about them. Participants were then asked to vote on the cards they would like to talk about. Each person was entitled to five votes (the FunRetrospectives board gives you the option to limit the number of votes per participant).

Checkout – One Word Before Leaving

To end the retrospective, as a checkout activity, we performed two actions:

1. We read the action items (a shared document was created during the retrospective and items were added during conversations about the top voted ones).

2. Each participant wrote a word that reflects how they felt at the time when the retrospective meeting ended. We used the *One Word Before Leaving* from *FunRetrospectives*.

FunRetrospectives

One Word Before Leaving

Team!

more confident

motivated

excited

calm

safe

confident

engaged

Remote communication

Many of the images shared in this book show remote boards. As much as face-to-face meetings are preferred, remote work is a reality for many teams, as it was for our team.

Illustration based on a photo of the team in a Zoom meeting

There are several tools that facilitate remote communication, but nothing replaces face-to-face interaction between people. This team used Slack for everyday conversations, Zoom for meetings and telepresence, and *FunRetrospectives* for remote retrospectives. We had a Zoom meeting open all day, streaming what was happening in the team's area and, when someone needed to clear any doubts, they just had to unmute the microphone and speak. Even with these tools, the need to have more frequent face-to-face contact emerged in the retrospective.[38]

---

38 Note that the history of the team described in this book predates COVID19. However, this team already mixed remote and face-to-face work. Perhaps very similar to the working style of many teams today.

>> *DIA 38* **DAILY SCRUM PIGGY BANK**

This is a common practice for many product teams. The context: that typical five-minute delay in starting a meeting. The problem is, that's not fine at all, especially in a ten- to fifteen-minute meeting where people stand.

This is how the idea of a piggy bank - to collect the fine (typically a penny for every minute late) from anyone arriving late for the Daily Scrum — came about.

Here is the email instituting the Daily Scrum piggy bank:

Hi, all.

We changed our Daily standup time to have less delays/absences and, as suggested by the PO, we will now have to pay a small fee when we are late or absent from team meetings. :)

The idea is to reevaluate this practice and the amount of money in our piggy bank after we've been doing it for a while. The sponsor's presence will be agreed upon as required, however, for the rest of the team this is valid for daily scrum, planning, review, and retrospective meetings.

Initially, I will be responsible for controlling the money in a shared spreadsheet. If you have any questions or feedback, please contact me.

Mary.

» DAY 38 ANOTHER DAILY STANDUP – THE KANBAN ON TRELLO

Note in the image below the remote team using the Trello board on their Daily Scrum meeting. They were following the Top-to-bottom Daily Scrum style.

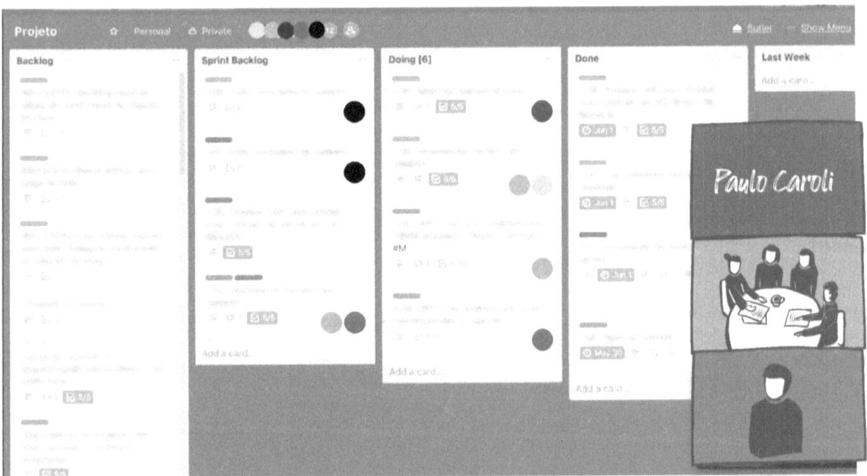

The team talks about the stories in the doing column. For example, on one of the cards, the developer opened it and said: "Yesterday I finished this story, this, that and this other thing happened. But the story is complete according to the acceptance criteria. I'm moving it to the done column".

The team uses a To do > Doing > Done style kanban, in which the To do column represents the worklist for the Sprint, the Sprint backlog as agreed in the Sprint Planning.

>> DAY 39 DEVOPS ASSESSMENT CURRENT STATE

As previously planned, we went through the DevOps assessment one more time. In the third week, the assessment was used to check the status of the legacy, of the code that the team received. This was noted in the "Legacy DevOps Assessment" chapter.

Importantly, both the questions asked, and the people interviewed were the same.

Below you will find an image and a table demonstrating the results for each assessment domain in the beginning of Sprint 1 (one week after Lean Inception) and Sprint 4 (four weeks after Lean Inception).

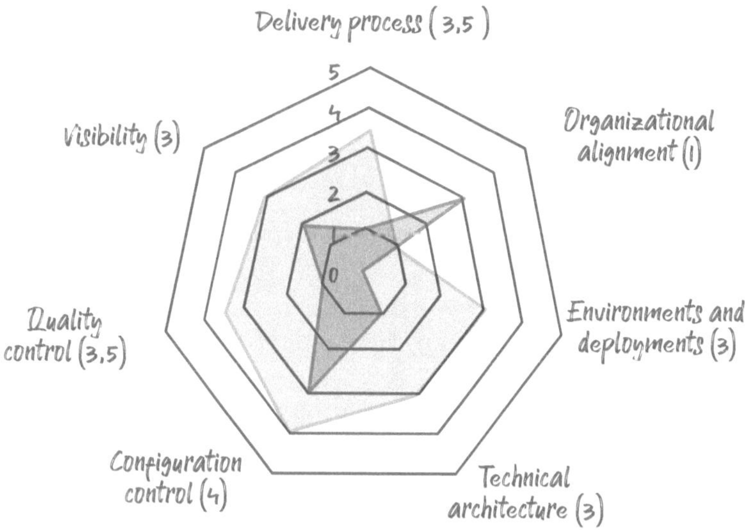

DOMAIN	GRADE SPRINT 1	GRADE SPRINT 4
Delivery process	1	3,5
Quality control	1	3,5
Configuration control	3	4
Environments and deployments	0	3
Data storage	NA*	NA*
Technical architeture	1	3
Organizational alignment	3	1
Visibility	2	3

* NA = Not applicable

Below you will find the notes and comments from the interviewees.

Delivery process – Legacy

Grade: 1

> There was a pattern of branches (gitflow style) and there was a manual test, when an ok came back, the artifacts were sent by email.

Delivery process – Current

Grade: 3,5

> We now have automated tests that run on every commit.

Quality control – Legacy

Grade: 1

> Android project didn't have any kind of tests; iOS project had a few unit tests.

> Manual tests were performed on each product release.

> It's the support team that tracks bugs.

Quality control – Current

Grade: 3,5

> Previously, only a manual test performed by the support team was used; we now test manually and automatically before it goes into production.

Configuration control – Legacy

Grade: 3

> Both Android and iOS projects already used the dependency manager – Gradle and Cocoapots. They already used Git.

Configuration control – Current

Grade: 4

> We are starting to move towards trunk-based, but we are not there yet. All testing, environment set-up scripts are in Git, our version control.

Environments and deployments – Legacy

Grade: 0

> We don't have a complete test environment (there is a QA01 for the back-end, but no mobile test environment).

> We don't have CI. Every deployment process is manual (with APK back and forth via email).

Environments and deployments – Current

Grade: 3

> We have the QA01 test environment that still doesn't work; but we now have mocked test environments. We currently have releases via script.

Data storage

Grade: not applicable

> Our product is just middleware, no database.

Technical architecture – Legacy

Grade: 1

> The code is tightly coupled, we don't have anything automated. It is very difficult to unit test the code. But version-based dependency management already exists.

Technical architecture – Current

Grade: 3

> I don't remember what I put as a technical architecture grade for the legacy, but I would say it should be a 0. Now it's a 3 because we have frequent conversations about architecture. In everyday life we discuss testing strategy, refactoring and how to isolate features. But given the current state of the code, we still have to improve.

Organizational alignment – Legacy

Grade: 3

> There is an open channel for communication with the product teams (which consume our SDK).

> There is a bit of knowledge separation: one person knows Android, another knows iOS.

Organizational alignment – Current

Grade: 1

> The alignment between what we are doing, and business needs is not clear. The initial plan we talked about at Lean Inception has changed, but we're not sure what the current plan is.

Visibility – Legacy

Grade: 2

> We have the release history on Git.
> The team started using Trello to give visibility to their work.

Visibility – Current

Grade: 3

> We were able to track who did what, as this is in Trello and GitLab. But we don't know when a version goes into production, as dates and deliverables aren't clear to everyone on the team.

>> DAY 39 MEETING TO PRESENT THE DEVOPS ASSESSMENT

The best benefit of the DevOps Assessment is not the assessment itself, but the conversation generated from it.

We set up a meeting with everyone on the team and our main sponsors to present the assessment and talk about the next steps regarding DevOps.

In addition to the people on the team and the main sponsors, a DevOps Coach (a senior consultant with experience in DevOps culture and practices) was also attending this meeting. He was present, as the client expressed interest in adding a consultant during some Sprints to pair up with developers and coach them on DevOps and software engineering practices (tests, automation, continuous delivery, etc.).

Here are some of the next steps the DevOps Coach will work on:

» Give visibility to the proportion of bugs per release (in order to check if increased stability leads to fewer bugs).

» Add an alert to the continuous integration server for when the percentage of tests drops below the minimum level determined for each component (in our case an SDK).

» Foster the practice of feature flag and decouple the deployment from the release (Reduce dependency and synchronism between the business and the team).

» Promote Dark launch and blue-green deployment practices.

» Analyze in detail our product data storage, considering the local base and the need for testing data.

» Create and give visibility to versioning with automatic notification of new releasable candidates (essential for our team and for all teams that use our product – SDK).

» Create a dashboard for installing and using our product (for example, we need to know when the first user makes use of an application with our SDK).

>> DAY 40 RETROSPECTIVE INVITATION

Team,

Here are the links and agenda to prepare for our retrospective today.

1. **Context:** We are in Sprint 4. Let's talk about achievements and improvements, given our learning so far.

2. **Prime directive for retrospectives:** "Regardless of what we discover, we understand and truly believe that everyone did the best job they could, given what was known at the time, their skills and abilities, the resources available, and the situation at hand."

3. **Energizer:** Surprise.

4. **Check-in:** Let's use the *Safety Check* activity. Please use this board from *FunRetrospectives*.

5. **Main course:** Let's use the *FLAT* activity (*Future direction, Lessons learned, Accomplishments and Thank you*). Please use this board from *FunRetrospectives*.

6. **Filtering:** Each participant has five votes. The cards will be sorted by the most voted and we'll talk about them.

7. **Checkout:** We'll talk at the end of the retrospective.

Cheers,

Caroli and Mary pairing up.

» *DAY 40* **THE RETROSPECTIVE WAS CANCELED**

Here is the email sent after the retrospective was canceled due to lack of quorum.

Team,

We hear you and understand the rush of daily work, and canceling the retrospective is an indicator that we are operating reactively rather than proactively. For example, the fire department that spends so much time putting out fires that it can't work to prevent future fires.

Our team has a retrospective every two weeks. So, by canceling today's, we will have four weeks between retrospectives, a very long period for a product team that seeks continuous improvement. By no means do we want to add more meetings to everyone's busy schedule, we're just noticing many fires starting in our day-to-day.

This is likely a conversation beyond the scope of the team, considering the organizational dynamics. We leave here a question for reflection: How to change the operating model of our fire department?

Cheers,

Caroli and Mary pairing up.

MAIN PROBLEMS AND RECOMMENDATIONS

>> THE RESULT OF THE SIX WEEKS

The Agile consulting work carried out during the team's first six weeks was intended to:

- >> Conduct a Lean Inception to align the team in relation to the product that would be built.
- >> Facilitate the definition of team agreements, that is, how the team would work together.
- >> Support the team in the search for technical excellence.
- >> Support the delivery of the MVP.
- >> Identify pain points, bottlenecks, dependencies, and perceived issues.
- >> Align with the main stakeholders on the findings and how we would act on them.

The findings were presented to the stakeholders in the sixth week and the main problems and recommendations addressed in this conversation are listed below.

>> AMBIGUITY/DUALITY OF ROLES

The first point discussed at the meeting was the ambiguity and duality of some roles. In this case, the roles of Scrum Master, Product Owner and Engagement Manager.

Engagement Manager or Scrum Master?

In Porto Alegre, there were five developers and an Engagement Manager/ Scrum Master. At the client, in another city, there were two other developers, a UX Designer and a Product Owner.

As this was a consulting engagement, the role of Engagement Manager was necessary to carry out management tasks, and the role of Scrum Master was essential for the team. Having a person performing both roles was confusing to the team, mainly because that person did not have mandate to effectively play the role of Scrum Master in the client's organization.

In light of this finding, we created action items to ensure that Mary, as an external consultant, would have mandate to solve problems in which it was necessary to access people from other areas within the client's organization.

What is expected of the role of Product Owner?

It was also identified that there were different expectations for the role of Product Owner. The team expected a range of behaviors and activities, while the

PO had another view on the purpose of this role. The team's expectations were passed on to the PO. He shared his difficulties in meeting some of these perspectives and we reached an alignment on how we would proceed working in this context.

As an action item, it was defined that we would use a practice called Roles and responsibilities,[39] which aims to map out the responsibilities among the team roles. It helps them better define their roles and responsibilities and based on that, define what will or will not be part of each role within that context for that team.

---

39 Roles and Responsibilities. FunRetrospectives. Available at: https://www.funretrospectives.com/roles-and-responsibilities/. Accessed on: March, 2023.

CANCELED MEETINGS AND INTERRUPTED CADENCE

The second issue addressed in the conversation with stakeholders was the cancelation of team meetings and the impact that interrupting this cadence had on the team and on the engagement.

The Daily Scrum should always take place at the same time and place to reduce the complexity involved in having to find out what time the meeting is and where it will take place for each day of the week.

The problem here is that a good part of the team was preparing to participate in the Daily Scrum, going to the meeting room on time; turning on the equipment for the videoconference, joining the Zoom meeting and there was no sign of the rest of the team. The piggy bank helped at first, but after a while the problem recurred.

In addition to the delays and absences that occurred in the Daily Scrum, this also happened with the other team meetings: planning, review, and retrospective. These absences usually resulted in cancelations, and at other times the PO canceled the meeting due to other priorities.

We had already changed the meeting times twice to better serve the availability of all the people on the team and, at that time, we sought to answer the following questions: Why is this still happening? What is causing this delay?

By putting everyone in a room to discuss the problems together, it was possible to identify what was really behind the cancelations. Unknowingly, the sponsor was pulling people to other meetings at the same time; this was mainly the case with the PO. Not being aware of the impact this had on the engagement, the sponsor believed that this action was not a problem and did so without the slightest intention of harming the team.

We also found out in this conversation that many times the sponsor made a request to developers thinking that the matter in question was something simple and that they would spend a few hours to solve it. The reality was that these people sometimes went days without dedicating themselves to the engagement and this also caused meetings to be canceled.

The action item in this case was to identify in which situations it was necessary to assign people to other initiatives and meetings and seek alternatives to solve the problem, shielding the team. We also agreed that we would give the sponsor visibility of the impact that necessary absences would generate on the expected outcomes, so that decisions could be made in a conscious way.

>> ONE WEEK SPRINTS WITH FORTNIGHTLY RETROSPECTIVES

The team decided to work with one-week Sprints, however with a retrospective every two weeks. This was a decision the team made in the second week of work, in the first retrospective, in an activity to define the team agreements.

> *"Every team must do one retrospective per week unless they are out of time. In that case they must do two!"*

Caroli always repeats that phrase. We even sent this to the team in an email about the importance of retrospectives.

During the Defining the Team Agreements activity (on day 12), the team decided to do a retrospective every two weeks. We talked about it and we both, Mary and Caroli, preferred frequent retrospectives, but as this was a team decision, we complied.

However, a few weeks later, we regretted it. The retrospective, as a continuous improvement meeting, took place at a frequency far below the needs of this newly formed team.

Precisely because the team is being established, it needed to align several important aspects such as expected behaviors and ways of working in order to deliver efficiently.

But there were no retrospectives, no other meeting or forum to talk about improvements. There weren't enough moments to establish the team's agreements, or to readjust the understanding given new discoveries.

We understand that unforeseen events happen and sometimes meetings are canceled. That was the case with a retrospective meeting. In that case, the team would go four weeks without one. However, as we had important challenges to be resolved, we had to schedule on-demand meetings to deal with the challenges we were facing at that time.

It would have been easier and with less intervention (email asking for an extra meeting, as it wasn't on everyone's agenda), if we had weekly retrospectives, instead of fortnightly with cancelation.

Our suggestion is that this team maintain the cadence of one week Sprints, but with one retrospective per week. That way we can deal with problems while these are still small, and this will also reduce the need for emergency meetings. And it still includes the exceptional case that a retrospective is canceled (we don't recommend this, but if it does happen, the team won't go more than two weeks without this extremely important meeting for continuous improvement). So we recommend having a retrospective per Sprint, that is, one every week. The delivery cycle is weekly, so the retrospective must be in this same cycle.

>> TOO MANY SPIKES AND LACK OF BUSINESS DIRECTION

During the first six weeks of the engagement, a high number of spikes (technical investigation to make decisions) per Sprint was observed and the difficulty in defining what we were looking to discover with these spikes often caused them to generate new spikes.

This was causing a lot of anxiety on the team. The PO thought the team was too slow as we still hadn't delivered anything tangible. Developers, on the other hand, did not see progress in the face of so much uncertainty and felt frustrated with the work.

Once again, we tried to understand the source of the problem, and having the right people in the same room was essential.

With the absence of the PO, some business decisions were not taken, and the lack of direction caused the team to explore all possible options for all problems. This situation was heightened when the PO delegated these responsibilities to a developer who had been working with the product from the beginning. This developer understood very well about the how, but he didn't have the vision of the users and the business.

The result of this was the excess of spikes that sought to explore different ways of doing something, but that were not related to any business objective.

Being fully transparent, we aligned expectations with the PO and stakeholders about who would make the decisions and give business direction. As an action item of this topic, we scheduled a workshop in Porto Alegre with the whole team to define OKRs (the chapter "Objectives and key results - OKR," at the beginning of this book, explains more about the subject) and plan the team objectives for the coming months.

>> LACK OF VISIBILITY ABOUT THE TEAM'S HEALTH

When we tried to identify what was causing discomfort in the team and what needed to be improved, we realized that one of the problems was precisely the lack of visibility about its health.

Despite the various mechanisms we used to bring people together, this environment only allowed us to notice that the climate was not good or that there was a problem. There was still a lack of information about what could be harming the team's health.

In addition, it was very difficult to make the problems visible to the rest of the team that was located in another city. It was also difficult to feel what the climate was like over there. We needed to do more than just guessing.

To check the team's health, we suggest periodic monitoring (in each Sprint, if possible) of the following aspects: people, processes, and product. Each of these aspects represents a third of the team's wheel, with the colors green, yellow and red, respectively representing a good situation, one that requires some attention, and one that requires corrective action with greater urgency.

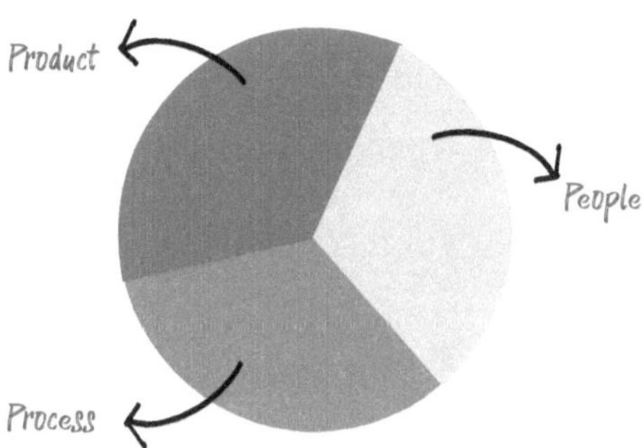

Below is a list of questions for each aspect. These questions should be used to determine the right color (status): green, yellow or red.

People

> Do we need more people on the team, either to complement it with some necessary knowledge or role, or to increase its capacity?

> Are there too many people on the team? Do we have too much idle capacity?

> Was the onboarding of new people on the team well planned and executed?

> Was the roll-off of people on the team well planned and executed?

> Do we have relationship problems between people?

> Is everyone happy and effective with their current role and work on the team?

Process

> Do all the people on the team, as well as their stakeholders and sponsors, understand and agree with the process currently used?

> Do all participants and people interested in the team's work know where and how to look for information about it (where it is, how it is going, where it is going, why)?

> Does everyone on the team understand and agree on the relationship between product scope, delivery dates and team capacity?
> Does everyone understand their role on the team and know how to work with people who play other roles?

Product

> Does everyone understand the strategic direction of the product?
> Does everyone understand the product's metrics and how each new feature is being measured?
> Does everyone understand the features, stories and tasks being created and how these relate to the product and its release schedule?
> Is the pace of completing work items consistent with the scope commitment and delivery date for the product (or MVP) in question?

≫ SHARED PEOPLE AND
LOW PRIORITY

Given the business context, the people who were allocated on the client side were not exclusive to this team, that is, they worked on two or more products at the same time. From the beginning there was a lot of conversation about how we could get these people 100% dedicated to this product, but this change was simply not possible in the short term, and we had to work with that restriction.

Many of the problems discussed above occurred or were enhanced for this reason. Of all, this was the issue that impacted the team the most, and the fact that the other initiatives were treated with higher priority intensified the issue even further.

What we asked during the conversation with stakeholders was: What determines the priority of the initiatives? Does this engagement really have low priority? We found that, in fact, this engagement was the most important one, but since this alignment had not been done internally, the loudest voices were determining the priority. We then talked about the impacts the product had on the organization and sought to raise awareness among stakeholders about this importance.

Although listed as an issue related to the engagement, this situation went beyond and was too complex to be handled by the team alone. It was a problem already known and intrinsic to the way the organization works, that is, it was part of the company's culture.

At that time, we knew that we would not solve the problem during the engagement, with this team, but transparency was very important to align expectations and manage conflicts.

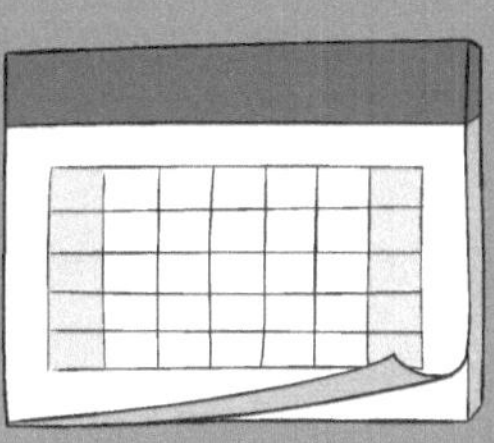

THE NEXT FOUR MONTHS

» I'M SEEING. I'M HEARING

Something simple that often goes unnoticed: it is very important to see and hear people. This generates empathy and simple, straightforward communication.

However, this team was split between two cities. The good thing is that they were already used to working remotely. The team communicated daily by Slack, email, WhatsApp group, board in Trello, board in FunRetrospectives, Zoom meetings, etc.

Luckily, we had a Lean Inception in the very first week of work, where everyone was together for a week in the same city. Collaborative work during the Lean Inception generated a lot of empathy and a good initial relationship.

But the day-to-day communication, while each person was sitting in their chair, could be improved. And it was!

A simple technique, but one that brings people even closer: A big screen with the microphone muted and the video, camera, and audio on, placed in each of the locations.

Now, when a person wants to check why someone hasn't responded to an email, if they have already gone to the meeting room, or haven't arrived at work yet, they simply look at the screen and confirm: "oh, she is not there, sitting in her chair." But if they see the person there, "remotely beside them" (on the screen), just unmute the microphone and talk to her.

As simple as that, it was possible to make half of the team that was in an office in city A and the other half that was in another office in city B, to be "in the same room"![40]

One of the XP practices — eXtreme Programming — favors that the team should be together, all seated at a single table. This practice called *Colocated team* is even common in more agile companies, but it was a very extreme idea in 1999.

Since we cannot be together physically, we must be together remotely. Keep a channel with video and audio on to create the concept of Colocated teams for remote teams.

---

40 This solution worked well back then. There are now some excellent apps that can do the same thing. Check out toucan.events and KosyOffice.com.

WHO FACILITATES THE SCRUM MEETINGS ?

The developers who were located in Porto Alegre already had experience with Scrum and were interested in developing facilitation skills. This combination was the perfect reason for us to try a different way of working when the opportunity came up.

During a conversation about expectations for the Scrum Master role, we agreed that facilitating Scrum meetings shouldn't be the responsibility of the person in that role alone, and from that came the idea of putting together a facilitation schedule. We used sticky notes to create the schedule on a whiteboard where the team was located.

The facilitation schedule worked as follows:

We were six people in Porto Alegre, and we worked five days a week. So we decided that we would pick a different person for each day of the week, and someone would be off, not doing any facilitation work, every week. In the beginning of each week, we rotated people so that whoever had been off the week before was now responsible for facilitating the Monday meetings. This ensured that everyone would have the opportunity to facilitate all types of meetings.

Having someone "off-duty" helped because when someone needed to go on vacation, it was just a matter of agreeing to swap with whoever was supposed to be off-duty during that period. Managing this schedule and ensuring that a facilitator would always be present was the responsibility of the entire team and not just the person in the Scrum Master role.

Often there were some activities and action items that needed developers, but no one volunteered to do them. Some examples: putting together a presentation on TDD for the client, documenting test guidelines, ensuring that the feedback when pair programming was happening, among others.

In search of a solution to this problem, the facilitation schedule gained one more purpose. Whenever an activity came up that no one wanted to do, the facilitator of the day would be responsible for it.

This worked very well throughout the engagement, and when someone was working from home, the common question on the team's Slack was: "Who is the facilitator today?".

THE FIRST RELEASE IN PRODUCTION

The time has come to put the MVP into production!

The team's first challenge with this release was the long time that passed from the beginning of the engagement until the first release actually went into production. It took more than three months. But if the team worked with one week Sprints, that is, delivered product increments every week, why did it take so long to have something in production?

Due to the problems presented in the previous chapter: the lack of definition of the PO's role, canceled meetings, excessive spikes, lack of business direction, lack of visibility about the team's health, people being shared across multiple teams, the lack of retrospectives and, mainly, the low priority of the engagement. All these issues influenced a lot so that the first release took so long, but that wasn't all.

The main lesson learned was the importance of continuous integration. As we were working with an SDK, we delivered our product increments to other teams that were responsible for integrating our SDK with their respective products.

For over three months we've delivered patches and added a lot of new features to our product. A lot of integration testing was done, but the SDK was never really integrated with any product during all this time. It is obvious that when the time came for this to happen, there were many problems.

The risk was raised in several daily Scrum meetings, planning meetings, reviews, and retrospectives, but we could not prioritize this integration in other teams' backlogs. Sometimes you have to feel the pain first and then do something about it, and that's exactly what happened here.

After the release, we did a two-hour retrospective where we understood all the points where we went wrong so that the same mistakes were not made in the next releases. The main action item was: "Set dates with other teams for product integration before releases."

≫ TEAM AGREEMENTS

After the MVP went into production, we stopped to review our ways of working and to make some agreements on how we would work from that point forward.

Team agreements

- » Avoid moving cards backwards on the board.
- » Respect the WIP Limit.
- » Keep kanban updated (& do not work on things that are not on the board).
- » Tag cards that are in progress for over a week.
- » Use the Definition of Ready and Definition of Done checklists.
- » Measure the flow.
- » No "mouse" (too small) or "elephant" (too big) stories.

At this point we were already using Kanban and we weren't doing Sprint Planning and Sprint Review anymore. We continued with weekly retrospectives and the daily meeting started to work in a different way. The main question now was: "What is needed for this card to move to the next stage?".

» INDIVIDUALS AND INTERACTIONS OVER PROCESSES AND TOOLS

Practices, techniques, ceremonies, and tools do not work alone! People must understand what they are for and when to use them. Furthermore, with an understanding of the values and principles, it is possible to adapt them to the right context and take greater advantage of their application. The essence of this work, which took place Sprint by Sprint, was in the values and principles of the Agile Manifesto. And that was what made it possible to understand what was not working so that we could change course.

While building the MVP, several agile practices were used. We constantly applied agile principles and worked on the continuous improvement of the pillars: people, technology, and processes. However, something still didn't seem to work very well. In the constant search for continuous improvement, we reflected on the first value of the Agile Manifesto, which says: "Individuals and interactions over processes and tools." By putting this value into practice, it was possible to understand that, in addition to adopting agile practices, it was necessary to improve interaction between people.

No matter how hard you try to use the best processes and tools, the success of the team and, consequently, of the product, depends much more on people and their interactions. Given this realization, it was necessary to take a step back, review the team composition and how we were interacting within and outside the team. Making these changes was fundamental to transforming a group of people into a high performing team!

APPENDIX

» TEMPLATES

The following are some of the templates that were created during the engagement presented in this book.

Definition of Ready Checklist

Each work item (stories, tasks, etc.) candidate for the Sprint Planning must pass this checklist. A negative answer indicates that the item is not ready to go into planning.

☑ Item ready for the Sprint Planning

Do I have the information I need to do the work?

☐ No

☐ Yes, please specify:

Do I know why we need this work item?

☐ No

☐ Yes, please specify:

Do I know how to show the completion of this work item?

☐ No

☐ Yes, please specify:

Can I relate this work item to an epic or expected outcome?

☐ No

☐ Yes, please specify:

Does this work item fit in a Sprint?

☐ No, item must be broken into smaller units

☐ Yes

Sprint Backlog Checklist

Use this checklist at the end of your Sprint Planning meeting. In case of any negative answer, talk to the team about the reasons. If necessary, resolve the issue before it impacts the Sprint.

Does the team have the knowledge to work on the items that are in the Sprint Backlog?

☐ No

☐ Yes, please specify:

Was the Sprint goal defined and understood? Is it relevant and achievable?

☐ No

☐ Yes, please specify:

Does the Sprint backlog generate a product increment of value to the user?

☐ No

☐ Yes, please specify:

Does the amount of work take into account the WIP limit, capacity and team calendar?

☐ No

☐ Yes, please specify:

Is the team confident we can achieve the Sprint goal?

☐ No

☐ Yes, please specify:

Definition of Done Checklist

The team agrees that a work item (story, task, etc.) is done if they can cross off all the items on this checklist. If not, it means that the item is not complete yet.

Does this work item deliver an increment of the product?

☐ No

☐ Yes, please demonstrate:

Does it meet the acceptance criteria?

☐ No

☐ Yes, please demonstrate:

Is it documented?

☐ No

☐ Yes, please demonstrate:

Does it follow the coding and technical standards?

☐ No

☐ Yes, please demonstrate:

Is it within the product performance thresholds?

☐ No

☐ Yes, please demonstrate:

WIP considerations

Before adding more items to the Sprint backlog, let's check the current status of the items in progress (WIP). After considering how much work we believe is still outstanding to complete these items, we decide how much to add to the Sprint and set its goal.

Sprint goal setting considerations

Before we decide on the work items for this Sprint, let's first talk about its goal.

The Sprint Goal is a brief description of the Sprint's purpose. For example: a specific business problem to be solved or a grouping of related functionalities. Typically, work during the Sprint is adjusted and aligned with the target of reaching your goal.

Imagine this scenario: A director comes to a developer and asks, "I need you to create a report to show the number of contested sales last year by region." The developer should politely answer "How does this relate to the Sprint goal?" and find a way to get the attention of the PO and Scrum Master to help them stay focused on the goal.

If the team has a lot of WIP (work in progress) not yet finished from the last Sprint, the goal of the current one should be something like: "The same as the last Sprint, because we haven't reached it yet, which is [insert goal from the previous Sprint here]."

Idea Validation Template

We believe that _________________ (this MVP)

will achieve _________________ (these expected outcomes).

We will know that this happened based on _________________

_________________ (metrics to validate business hypotheses).

MVP Canvas

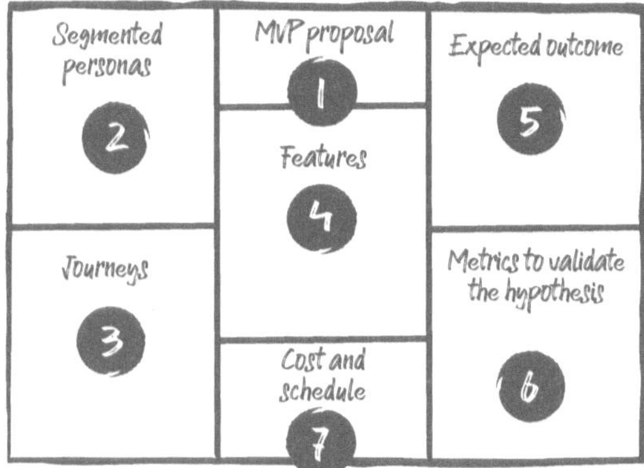

Here is the recommended order when filling it out or thinking about the blocks:

1. **MVP proposal**: What is the purpose of this MVP?

2. **Segmented personas**: Who is this MVP for? Can we segment and test it on a smaller group?

3. **Journeys**: What journeys are completed or enhanced by this MVP?

4. **Features:** What are we going to build in this MVP? What actions will be simplified or improved by it?

5. **Expected outcomes:** What lesson or result are we looking for in this MVP?

6. **Metrics to validate business hypotheses:** How can we measure the outcomes of this MVP?

7. **Cost and schedule:** What is the cost and expected delivery date of this MVP? Once delivered, how long will we need to collect the data to decide whether to move away or move forward?

User Story template

User Story description

» *As a* _________________________ (role/profile) _________________________

» *I want* _________ (action to be performed/product-specific feature) _________

» *So that* _________________ (value achieved) _________________

Acceptance criteria

» *Given* _________________ (initial scenario) _________________

» *When* _________________ (action performed) _________________

» *Then* _________________ (expected state) _________________

OKR template

We will _________________ (objective) _________________ ,

as measured by _________________ (this set of key results) _________________ .

≫RETROSPECTIVE ACTIVITIES

In this chapter you can find the retrospective activities that were mentioned in the book. More details and activities can be found in the book *Funretrospectives*.

Ping Pong

This is a short activity to start the meeting in a good mood and get the participants engaged.

Step by step:

1. Start by saying the number 1 followed by the name of another participant.
2. The next person mentally adds 1 to the number. Then:
   > If the number is not a multiple of 3 or 5: the person says the number.
   > If the number is a multiple of 3: the person says ping.
   > If the number is a multiple of 5: the person says pong.

   And say someone else's name
3. Go back to the previous step. However, if anyone gets it wrong, start from number 1 again.

   For large groups, it is recommended to remove the person from the group if they make a mistake or wrongly accuse someone. Soon, everyone will be laughing and cheering for those who are still playing.

Isn't that Crazy

This activity is awesome for getting people talking and collaboratively creating a (usually funny) story. It promotes engagement and participation of all, being very easy to facilitate, as it is carried out verbally.

Step by step:

1. One person starts by saying "Isn't that crazy" and someone else's name.
2. The next participant should continue the story by adding three or four words and someone else's name.
3. And so on until someone says "End".

   Here is an example:

   "Isn't that crazy"

   "Those flying birds"

   "But I've seen it"

   "A flying cat"

   "And with superpowers"

   "With laser eyes"

   "That freezes mobile apps"

   "But not ours"

   "Because of Kryptonite"

This is a very fun and simple activity. Another variation is to start with "Once upon a time" and ask each person to add four words.

One Word

One Word is an activity used to check everyone's feelings before starting or closing a retrospective. It's usually a great time for people to share their feelings, especially when they're very excited about the retrospective.

Step by step:

1. Ask participants to describe their feelings in *One Word* on a Post-It and place it on the common board.

   "Please share a word that describes how you are feeling right now."

2. Ask if anyone wants to share more about the chosen word.

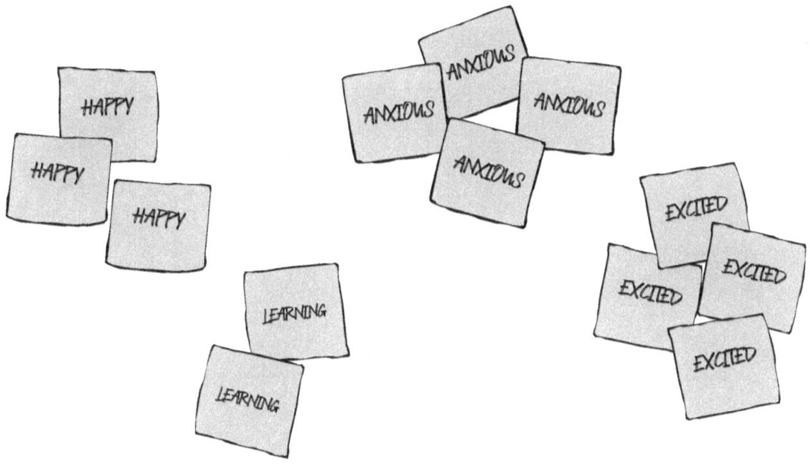

This activity is very simple, inspiring people to speak out-loud about how they feel at that moment in the retrospective.

Safety Check

This is a quick and effective way to measure group open participation in the retrospective activities.

Step by step:

1. Ask participants to choose a number between 1 and 5 that indicates how safe they feel within the group, and write them down on a Post-It (numbers must be collected anonymously, so everyone must use the same colors of sticky note and marker). Below, you can check the meaning of each number:

   5: No problem, I'll talk about anything.

   4: I will talk about almost everything, some subjects may be more difficult.

   3: I will talk about some things, but others will be difficult to say.

   2: I won't say much; I'll let the others raise the issues.

   1: I will smile, say everything is fine, and agree with the managers.

2. The facilitator collects sticky notes from each participant (use a hat or some container to keep it anonymous).

3. Make the result of the *Safety Check* visible to the whole group.

4. Confirm the results and decide what comes next.

Safety Check

What to do with the results?

What can be said when:

> The safety level is high: "It seems that many here in the room are willing to talk about many topics, so it's worth moving on to the next activity, which will spark a lot of conversation."

> The safety level is medium: "As seen in the results, some participants are not willing to talk about all topics. Let's keep that in mind, and I, as the facilitator, won't ask everyone's opinion as some of you aren't comfortable talking about everything."

> Safety level is low: "As seen from the results of the *Safety Check*, let's use the remaining time and do an activity that can help us increase the safety level of the group."

Creating Safety

This is a good follow-up activity when the safety level is low or medium. It allows participants to talk about anything that might make them uncomfortable. A low safety level compromises any meeting, so don't get stuck on your agenda if that's your case — work to create safety instead.

Step by step:

1. Ask for insights into what could be diminishing safety: "So, put yourself in someone's shoes who isn't feeling safe to talk about some issues. What could be the causes of this? Please write them on a yellow sticky note and put it on the board." That phrase is very powerful. The *Safety Check* is anonymous, but the phrase opens the door for matters to be handled in a subtle way. The person does not have to say, "I feel unsafe because of this or that."

Instead, questions are raised without a first person. This should reveal the causes that decrease safety without revealing who isn't feeling safe.

2. Group the causes on the board by similarity.

3. Ask participants to provide ideas on how to make people feel safe, given the causes on the board: "Think about the things you can do to help tackle these causes on the board (on yellow sticky notes), write them on orange sticky notes and put them next to the cause."

4. Read all the notes and (carefully) lead a conversation about them. The facilitator will have to use their judgment when reading the notes and conducting the conversation. You should keep in mind that some people may be uncomfortable with some topics and ideas, so don't rush to conclusions or put people on the spot.

5. Do the *Safety Check* again.

If all goes well, the safety level will increase. What is important is that the results of the Safety Check have been taken into account and that the participants have the opportunity to talk about it with confidence.

Defining the team's agreements

This activity helps the team collectively define and write down the team agreements they want to have in place. It promotes an honest and democratic conversation about how the team should work.

Step by step:

1. Introduce the activity, adding more discussion areas if needed: "Let's talk about how we're going to interact with each other and work together.

Collectively, we will write the team agreements for each of these areas:"

> Purpose and agenda of meetings.

> Preferred method of communication.

> Roles and availability.

> Ways of working.

2. Divide the frame between the number of areas identified (in this example, four).

3. Ask for individual contribution. "Write your notes on the team's agreements for each identified area. You must use the sticky note color as per the annotation:

> Constraint (pink).

> Strong recommendation (green).

4. Chat with each other and take notes (consider writing action items on sticky notes of a different color).

Small Starfish

This is an adaptation of an activity known as Starfish. The Small Starfish is divided into three areas instead of five. It is a great data-gathering activity to foster reflection around practices and the value the team gets from them. It helps team members understand the perceived value each person sees in such practices.

Step by step:

1. Divide the canvas into three areas:

> Keep doing: something the team is doing well, and you recognize the value in it.

> Less / Stop: something being done; you see some value, but you rather reduce; either a little bit or all of it.

> More of: something that has already been done, and you believe it will bring more value if done even more.

2. Ask participants to individually write their notes on sticky notes for each of the areas.

3. Discuss the sticky notes with the group.

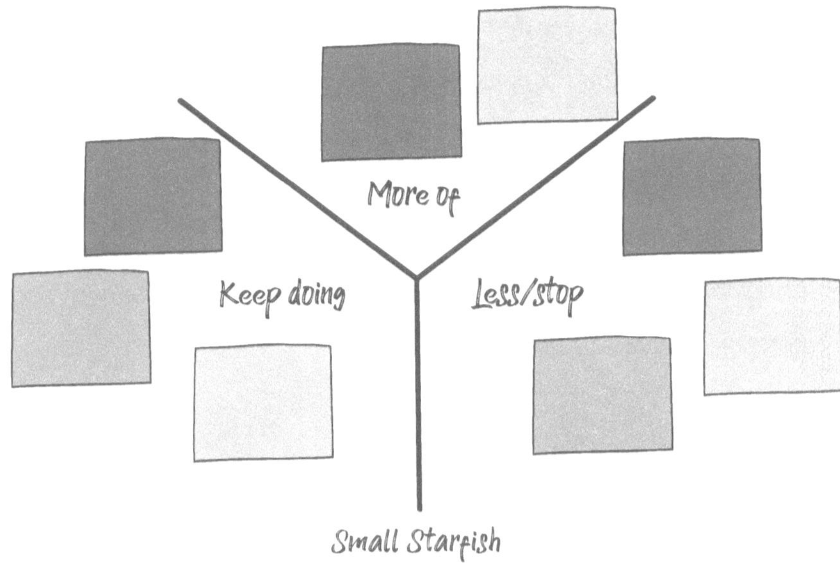

Timeline with Ups and Downs

This activity is also known as *Peaks and Valleys* or *Emotional Seismograph*. It promotes a simple visual language by sharing individual insights into the Ups and Downs of a given timeline. It is an effective way for a large group to view and discover events and their interconnections.

Step by step:

1. Draw a horizontal arrow representing the timeline at the bottom of the canvas. Define the beginning and end of the timeline.

2. Decide upon the canvas vertical gradient. For example, if it is the happiness gradient, then the top represents the happiest, and the bottom is the saddest.

3. Invite a participant to draw their Peaks and Valleys timeline:
"Starting on the beginning of the timeline, and keeping the marker on the canvas the whole time. Please share your Peaks and Valleys timeline. You should do so by drawing the line and speaking at the same time".

4. Invite more participants to draw their timeline (one at a time). Consider using a different marker color or line pattern.

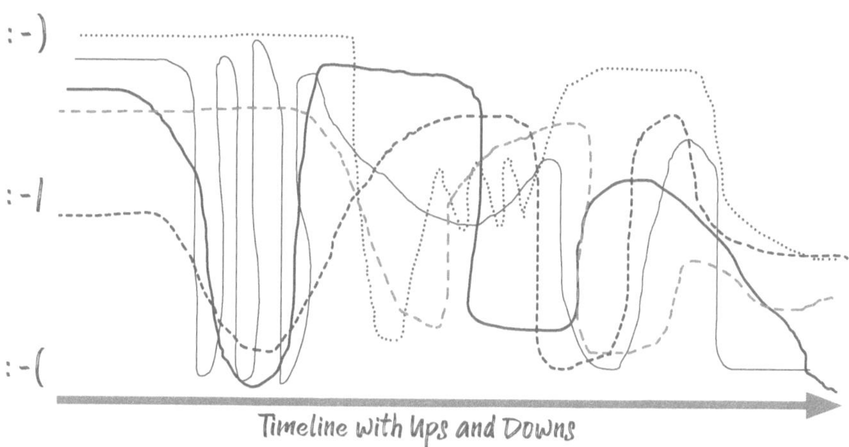

Timeline with Ups and Downs

At the end of this activity, the whole group will have a view of the timelines with ups and downs. It is a good activity for getting participants to open up for further conversation. It is also very useful for correlating events with the chosen gradient (team feelings on the example above) and for recognizing contradiction —such as ups and downs for the same event.

FLAP: Future direction, Lessons learned, Accomplishments and Problem areas

FLAP is a great project/phase postmortem activity. You should run it as close to the end of a project/phase as possible—don't wait or everyone will forget what happened.

Step by step:

1. Prepare and explain the FLAP canvas quadrants.

   > Future direction: write down all future directions regarding the project/phase.

   > Lessons learned: Write down the key lessons and takeaways from the project/phase.

   > Accomplishments: write down the key accomplishments for the project/phase.

   > Problem areas: Write down the problematic areas experienced throughout the specified project/phase.

2. Ask participants for their notes. Consider using color codes. For example, you can use a different color for each of the topics:

   > Processes and practices.

   > Technology and tools.

   > Scope and requirements.

   > People and teams.

3. Share the results and discuss them with the group.

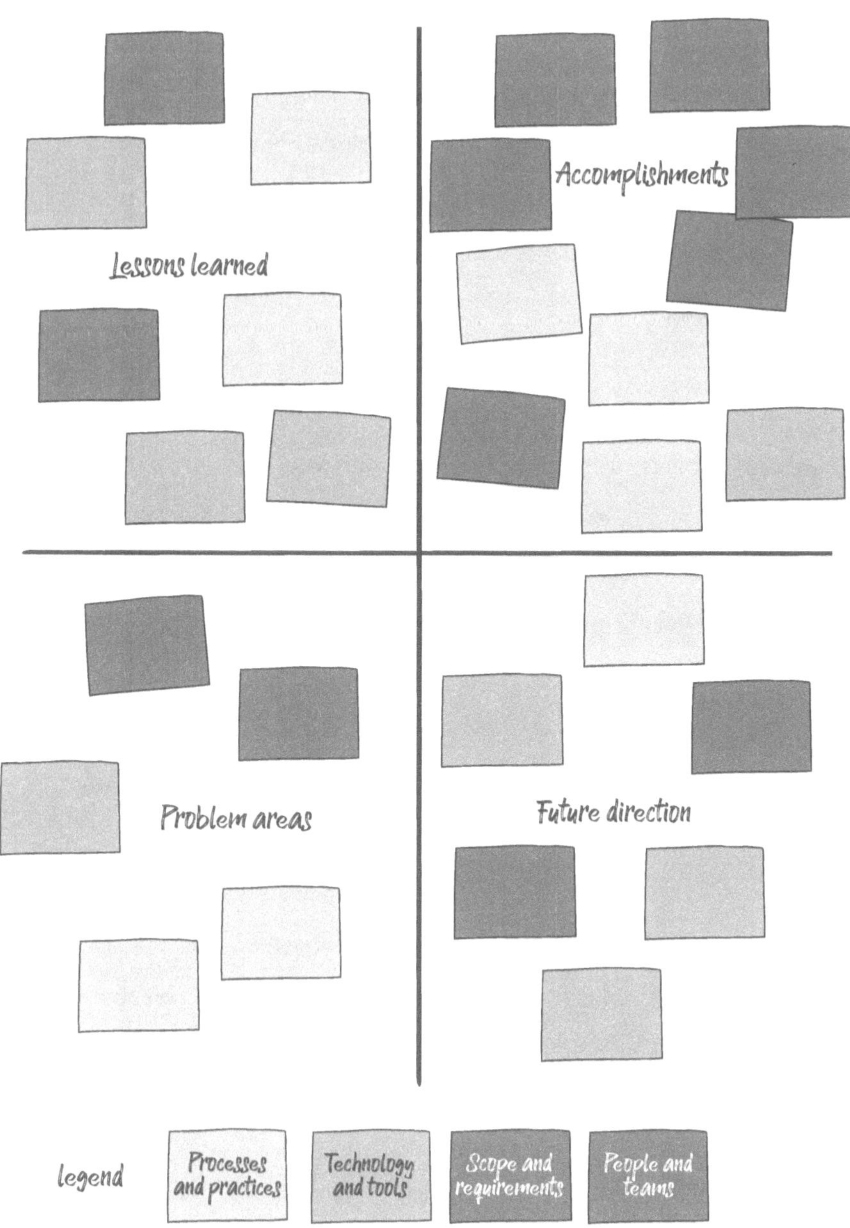

Lessons learned
Accomplishments
Problem areas
Future direction
legend
Processes and practices
Technology and tools
Scope and requirements
People and teams

Who-What-When

This activity helps define commitments and follow-up actions on meetings. Many meetings end with an unclear discussion about "next steps" or "action items". This activity avoids creating a list of tasks that are often handed out to possibly unwilling participants with no particular deadline attached.

Step by step:

1. Create a table structure that outlines WHO / WHAT / WHEN as column titles.
2. Ask participants to select (from previous activity) or write down a concrete step to which they can commit. These should be either (1) steps they are required to follow, or (2) steps they feel really strong about.
3. Each selected concrete step will form a row on the Who-What- When table. Ask participants to:
   > Place the sticky note with the step under the WHAT column.
   > Write the name of who is going to do the step in the WHO column.
   > Define WHEN the item will be done.

By focusing the discussion on a *Who-What-When* format, you can connect people with clear actions they defined and committed to. It enables participants to be clear about their commitments and responsibilities, making it visible to the whole group who will do what by when.

Note to Self

Note to Self is a very simple check-out activity. It focuses on the self, without any commitments to the group. Therefore, it is a good option after group conversations without clear group action items.

Step by step:

1. Ask participants to grab a marker and a sticky note.
2. Give them one minute to reflect upon the discussion that has just ended.
3. Ask each person to write a note to self about something they want to do and put it on their laptop as a reminder for the future.

While simple, writing a note and then reading it later on is a powerful way to get a person to think and then ponder (again) on something. Reflections are very personal and not everything needs to be a group discussion or group action items. We consider the note to self to be very powerful in fostering individual thoughts and reflections.

WHERE TO FIND MORE

n this book we shared the highs and lows of a product team in their journey to become a high-performing team. Some of the improvements you read about were possible after creating and using some artifacts, such as checklists.

On this page you will have access to some of the artifacts presented here (in pdf format, for easy downloading and printing).

https://caroli.org/en/livro/sprint-by-sprint/

JOIN THE SPRINT BY SPRINT TRAINING

In response to requests, we created a training course to complement the book. The Sprint by Sprint training addresses the different stages of a team and presents practices so that the team can be successful in becoming a high-performing team and achieving business outcomes. Check the training schedule at:

https://caroli.org/en/training/sprint-by-sprint/

Caroli.org, with an excellent team and the integration of authors, trainers, partners and other collaborators, is a company that seeks to share knowledge and, in this way, assist in the transformation of business, teams and organizations through agile and effective methodologies. We believe that new working relationships, with actionable ideas and teams aligned on the same purpose, can indeed contribute to the transformation of a better world.

Our content sharing happens in many ways, such as through articles on our blog, events with the community, exclusive and authorial trainings, and books written by the authors of the methods.

Visit our website www.caroli.org for more details. Other readers opted for the following books after finishing this one. Check out:

Align your team and begin the work in the agile way. *Lean Inception*, the step-by-step method for successful product teams.

Do you know what the main element of continuous improvement is? It is an effective and committed team. The *FunRetrospectives* book has the tools you need to develop it.

Build and refine your Product Backlog collaboratively, getting it ready for starting development, using the PBB (Product Backlog Building) canvas.

➡ ABOUT THE AUTHORS

Mary Provinciatto is passionate about innovation, product development, and continuous improvement. As a Product Leader, she helps organizations and teams overcome business and technology challenges by adopting the product operating model. She has solid experience in forming and leading product teams and worked with organizations from many different countries and industries, solving complex problems and delivering business value while focusing on principles over processes.

Mary gratuated from UNESP (São Paulo State University) in 2013 with a B.Sc. in Computer Science. She has an MBA in Project Management from FGV (Fundação Getulio Vargas) and an MBA in Marketing from ESPM (Escola Superior de Propaganda e Marketing).

She can be reached at:

maryprovinciatto.com

 @maryprovinc

 maryprovinciatto

 maryprovinciatto

Paulo Caroli is passionate about innovation, entrepreneurship, and digital products. He is a software engineer, author, speaker, and facilitator.

As principal consultant at ThoughtWorks and co-founder of Agile Brasil, Paulo has over twenty years of experience in digital product development, working for several corporations in Brazil, India, the United States, and countries in Latin America and Europe. In 2000, he discovered Extreme Programming and since then has focused his experience on agile & Lean processes and practices. He joined ThoughtWorks in 2006 and has held the positions of developer, Agile coach, trainer, project manager, and delivery manager. He holds a bachelor's degree in IT and a master's degree in software engineering, both from the Pontifical Catholic University of Rio de Janeiro (PUC-Rio).

Among his published books are *FunRetrospectives*; *Sprint by Sprint*, and the bestseller *Lean Inception*, which has now been published in five languages.

He can be reached at:

www.caroli.org

paulocaroli

Paulo.Caroli

➡ LEAVE YOUR REVIEW

f you got here, it's because you just read the book. Congratulations! Thank you so much for sharing and reading our content.

Authors live for the reviews they receive from readers. So if you enjoyed this book, we would be extremely happy to receive a 5-star rating for your reading!

If you have any criticisms, please send an email to paulo@caroli.org and let us know what to improve. That way we can add content and fix any errors so that your reading experience can be even better.

Thank you very much!

https://caroli.org/en/livro/sprint-by-sprint#rate